Edward de Bono

TEACH YOUR CHILD HOW TO THINK

VIKING

VIKING

Published by the Penguin Group
Penguin Books Ltd, 27 Wrights Lane, London W8 5TZ, England
Penguin Books USA Inc., 375 Hudson Street, New York, New York 10014, USA
Penguin Books Australia Ltd, Ringwood, Victoria, Australia
Penguin Books Canada Ltd, 10 Alcorn Avenue, Toronto, Ontario, Canada M4V 3B2
Penguin Books (NZ) Ltd, 182–190 Wairau Road, Auckland 10, New Zealand

Penguin Books Ltd, Registered Offices: Harmondsworth, Middlesex, England

First published 1992
1 3 5 7 9 10 8 6 4 2

Copyright © McQuaig Group Inc., 1992

The moral right of the author has been asserted

Set in 11/13 pt Lasercomp Melior
Printed in England by Clays Ltd, St Ives plc

A CIP catalogue record for this book is available from the British Library

ISBN 0–670–830135

Contents

PART THREE

PART FOUR

PART FIVE

PART ONE

My one ambition in writing this book is that around the world there should be a few more young people who come to say:

'I am a thinker.'

I would be even more pleased if some of them were to go further and say:

'I am a thinker – and I enjoy thinking.'

There is equal opportunity in this book for parents, and adults in general, to find themselves saying the same thing.

Thinking is not difficult. Thinking is not boring. You do not need to be a genius in order to be a good thinker.

The future well-being of the world is going to require good thinking. Personal life has always required good thinking but in the future the increasing complexity of demands and opportunities will require even better thinking. In business and professional life, good thinking is essential for survival, for success and for competition.

This Book is Not For You If . . .

1. You believe that intelligence is enough. If you believe that a highly intelligent person is automatically a good thinker and that a person with a lesser intelligence is less of a thinker, this book is not for you.

In my experience highly intelligent people are not always good thinkers. Many highly intelligent people fall into the 'intelligence trap' and function as poor thinkers.

Intelligence is a potential. Thinking is the skill with which we use that potential. I shall be discussing this point in more detail within a few pages.

2. You believe that thinking skills are already being taught in school. If you believe that school is the right place to teach thinking and that schools are doing this well, this book is not for you.

In my experience most schools do not teach thinking at all. Some schools teach the limited thinking skills involved in information sorting and analysis. Lately there has been something of a surge in the teaching of thinking in schools. Some schools have begun to teach 'critical thinking'. This is worthwhile but is also insufficient – and even dangerous – on its own (as I shall explain later).

The CoRT Thinking Program which I designed is now in use with millions of students in various countries around the world. Even so, it is unlikely to be in use in the school your children attend.

3. You believe that thinking skills cannot be taught directly. If you believe that thinking skills can be developed only by thinking about specific subjects or applying thinking in everyday life, this book is not for you.

Most people in education, and many others elsewhere, have always believed that thinking cannot be taught directly. This view is now beginning to change as experience and research begins to show that thinking skills can be taught directly.

Because we spend a lot of time thinking about things does not by itself improve our thinking skills. A journalist who types with two fingers will still be typing with two fingers at the age of sixty. This is not for lack of typing practice. Practice in two-finger typing will serve only to make that person a better two-finger typist. Yet a short course in touch typing at a young age would have made that person a much better typist for all his or her life. It is the same with thinking. Practice is not enough.

Introduction: Why We Need New Thinking About Thinking

INFORMATION AND THINKING

Information is very important. Information is easy to teach. Information is easy to test. It is not surprising that so much of education is concerned with information.

Thinking is no substitute for information but information may be a substitute for thinking.

Most theological definitions grant God perfect and complete knowledge. When knowledge is perfect and complete there is no need for thinking.

In some areas we might be able to achieve complete information and then those areas become routine matters that require no thinking. In the future we shall hand over these routine matters to computers.

Unless we have complete information we need thinking in order to make the best use of the information we have. When our computers and information technology give us more and more information we also need thinking in order to avoid being overwhelmed and confused by all the information.

When we are dealing with the future we need thinking because we can never have perfect information about the future.

For creativity, design, enterprise and doing anything new, we need thinking.

We need thinking in order to make even better use of information that is also available to our competitors.

So information is not enough. We do need thinking as well. Unfortunately there is a difficult dilemma. All information is valuable. Every new bit of information is of increasing value because it adds to what we already know. So how do we get the courage to reduce the amount of time we spend on teaching information in order to find time to teach the thinking skills that are needed to make the best use of the information? A trade-off is clearly needed.

INTELLIGENCE AND THINKING

The belief that intelligence and thinking are the same has led to two unfortunate conclusions in education:

1. That nothing needs to be done for students with a high intelligence because they will automatically be good thinkers.

2. That nothing can be done for students without a high intelligence because they cannot ever be good thinkers.

The relationship between intelligence and thinking is like that between a car and the driver of that car. A powerful car may be driven badly. A less powerful car may be driven well. The power of the car is the potential of the car just as intelligence is the potential of the mind. The skill of the car driver determines how the power of the car is used. The skill of the thinker determines how intelligence is used.

I have often defined thinking as: 'the operating skill with which intelligence acts upon experience'.

Many highly intelligent people often take up a view on a subject and then use their intelligence to defend that view. Since they can defend the view very well they never see any need to explore the subject or listen to alternative views. This is poor thinking and is part of the 'intelligence trap'.

In the diagram opposite we can see that one thinker sees the situation and instantly judges it. Another thinker sees the situation, then proceeds to explore the situation and only then proceeds to judge it. The highly intelligent person may carry out the 'seeing' and 'judging' very well indeed, but if the 'exploring' is absent that is bad thinking.

Highly intelligent people are usually good at solving puzzles or problems where all the pieces are given. They are less good at situations which require them to find the pieces and to assess the value of the pieces.

Finally there can be an ego problem. Highly intelligent people do

SITUATION

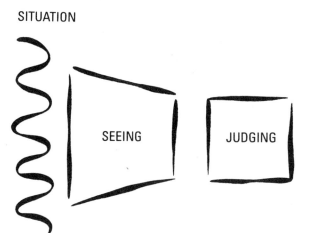

SITUATION

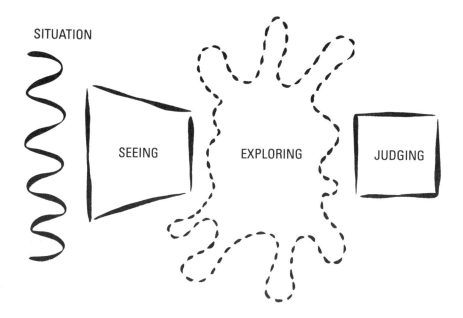

like to be right. This may mean that they spend their time attacking and criticizing others – since it is so easy to prove the others wrong. It also may mean that highly intelligent people are unwilling to take speculative risks because they cannot then be sure they are right.

There is, of course, nothing to prevent highly intelligent people also being excellent thinkers. But this does not follow automatically. There is need to develop the skill of thinking.

CLEVERNESS AND WISDOM

In school, in puzzles, in tests, in examinations and in our value-systems we put all the emphasis on cleverness.

A clever young man may make a great deal of money on Wall Street but his personal life may be a mess.

Cleverness is a sharp-focus camera lens: wisdom is a wide-angle lens.

We pay much less attention to wisdom than we do to cleverness. This is mainly because we believe that wisdom comes only with age and experience and that you cannot possibly teach wisdom. This is a fallacy. Wisdom can be taught. It is one of the main functions of this book to teach wisdom. Wisdom depends heavily on perception. It is a matter of teaching perception – not just logic.

DOES THINKING HAVE TO BE DIFFICULT?

Why do we always try to develop people's thinking by giving them tasks which are too difficult for them to do?

It is obvious that if the thinking task is too easy, there is no effort required, no sense of achievement, and nothing learned.

In almost all areas of skill development (tennis, skiing, music, cooking) we use tasks that are moderately difficult. In other words the tasks can be done, but as we do them we have to practise the skills we have. This builds up confidence and fluency in the skill. Tasks that are almost impossible destroy confidence. That is why so many people are turned off thinking. They find it boring because it is too difficult. There is no joy of performing if you cannot perform.

I do not believe that brain-teasers, puzzles and mathematical games are good ways to teach thinking. That is why the thinking tasks and exercises used in this book are not difficult.

Furthermore the belief that if you can do very difficult things then you can also do all things that are less difficult is not supported by human experience. Many people who are capable of very difficult mental feats sometimes seem less able to handle simpler tasks.

HOW TO BE AN INTELLECTUAL

The first rule of intellectualism is: 'If you do not have much to say, make it as complex as possible.' A true intellectual has as deep a fear of simplicity as a farmer has of droughts. If there is no complexity, what is there to work with or write about?

I have on occasion talked to audiences of educators who have more or less said: 'Please make your talk complicated enough for us to be impressed – but then it could be too complicated to be practical.'

There is no end to the complexity of descriptions. You could divide a simple pencil into ten parts if you wished and then proceed to describe all ten parts and the relationship of the parts. Once you have a handful of concepts you can choreograph the most complex of dances. There is no limit to the word games that can be played with words.

You comment on the complexity of others and also on the comments of commentators. And so the process feeds upon itself. Quite soon comment becomes more important than creativity and we esteem this as 'scholarship'.

Some people find this process unattractive and unnecessary. This is particularly true of those who are interested in practical outcomes. They come to equate 'intellectualism' with 'thinking' and get turned off thinking as a result. That is a pity.

You can be a thinker without being an intellectual. Indeed many intellectuals are not particularly good thinkers.

REACTIVE AND PRO-ACTIVE THINKING

In school it is very practical to put work-sheets, textbooks, and blackboard texts in front of students. The students are then asked to 'react' to what is before them. For these practical reasons almost all the thinking taught in school is 'reactive'.

'Here is something – what do you think of it?'

You cannot easily ask students to go out and organize a business. You cannot easily ask students to solve a real problem or undertake a real project. It simply is not practical in a school setting.

It also happens that this reactive type of thinking fits in with the intellectual tradition of scholarship: how do we react to what is already in existence?

But school and education is not a game unto itself. Real life involves a great deal of 'pro-active' thinking. This means going out and doing things. All the information is not given – you have to find it. Something is not placed before you. If you just sit in your chair nothing will happen. It is easy enough to eat in a restaurant if the meal is placed before you. But buying the food (or even growing it) and cooking it are different matters.

It is not the fault of education that pro-active thinking is not so easy to handle as reactive thinking. But it is the fault of education to suppose that reactive thinking is sufficient.

THE NEW WORD 'OPERACY'

Everyone knows what literacy and numeracy mean. I invented the word 'operacy' several years ago to cover the skills of 'doing'.

There is a myth in education that 'knowing' is enough. If you have sufficient knowledge, action is obvious and easy. If you have a detailed map, getting about is easy.

The real world is different. My many years of experience working with business and with government have shown that 'doing' is not at all easy. There is a great deal of thinking involved in doing. 'Gut feeling' and 'flying by the seat of the pants' have long ceased to be sufficient.

There are people to be dealt with. There are decisions to be made. There are strategies to be designed and monitored. There are plans to be made and implemented. There is conflict, bargaining, negotiating and deal-making. There are values to be assessed and trade-offs to be made. All this requires a great deal of thinking. All this requires a high degree of operacy.

In a competitive world, industrial nations that do not pay attention to operacy will be left behind. On a personal level, youngsters who do not acquire the skills of operacy will need to remain in an academic setting.

Operacy involves such aspects of thinking as: other people's views; priorities; objectives; alternatives; consequences; guessing; decisions; conflict-resolution; creativity and many other aspects not normally covered in the type of thinking used for information analysis. These things are part of 'pro-active' thinking, not the usual 'reactive' thinking.

CRITICAL THINKING

The traditions of Western thinking have put a very high emphasis on critical thinking. This is partly due to the ancient Greek habits of thinking that were rediscovered in the Renaissance, and partly due to the need for Church thinkers in the Middle Ages to have a way of attacking heresy.

Critical thinking has a high value in only two states of society. In a very stable society (as in the ancient Greek states and the Middle Ages) any new idea or intrusion that threatened change would need to be critically assessed. The second situation is when society is brimming with constructive and creative energy and critical thinking is needed to sort out the valuable from the spurious.

Unfortunately neither of these two states is present today. There is a tremendous need for change and there is a remarkable lack of new ideas and creative energy.

Imagine a project team of six brilliant critical thinkers who meet to discuss how they are going to cope with local pollution. None of them can use their highly trained minds until someone comes up with an actual suggestion. The difficulty is that critical thinking is 'reactive'. There has to be something to be 'criticized'. But where is that something going to come from? The proposals and suggestions have to come from thinking that is constructive and creative and generative.

If we trained a person to avoid all errors in thinking, would that person be a good thinker? Not at all. If we trained a car driver to avoid all errors in driving, would that person be a good driver? No, because that person could leave the car in the garage and so avoid any possibility of error. Avoiding errors in driving is very valuable provided the car is actually going somewhere. In the same way critical thinking is only valuable if we also have thinking that is constructive and creative. It is no use having reins if you do not have a horse.

This point is a very serious one because many schools believe that it is sufficient to teach critical thinking. They do this because it fits in with the usual emphasis on reactive thinking and also the traditional view of thinking.

Critical thinking is important and it does have a valuable place in thinking. But it is only a part of thinking. To say that a solitary wheel on a motor-car is inadequate is not to attack the worth of that wheel.

The dangers of believing critical thinking to be sufficient are many. The best brains become trapped in this sort of thinking and do not develop the constructive and creative thinking skills that are so essential for society. No time or effort in schools gets allocated to the constructive and creative aspects of thinking because the schools are deemed to be teaching 'thinking' already. There is the dangerous arrogance that can arise from critical thinking because thinking that is free of error is seen as being absolutely right – even though it is based on inadequate information or perception (I shall return to this point later). Skill in critical thinking without a matching skill in creative and constructive thinking makes it even more difficult for the needed new ideas to emerge. Criticism is very much easier than creation.

THE ADVERSARIAL SYSTEM

In the USA there is one lawyer for every 350 citizens.
In Japan there is one lawyer for every 9,000 citizens.
The adversarial system is fundamental to Western thinking traditions. It arises directly from the habits of critical thinking and the search for truth through adversarial dialogue.

Argument and debate are seen as the proper way to explore a subject because both parties are motivated. But as the motivation rises so the exploration falls. Would one party be inclined to bring forward a point which favoured the other side?

'I am right – you are wrong.'

The adversarial system is the basis of politics, law, science (to some extent), and daily life. Yet it is a very limited and defective system (this point is much more fully explored in my book *I Am Right – You Are Wrong**).

Polarities, polemics and conflicts are often made worse by the adversarial habit. Conflicts more often require a 'designed' outcome than a trial of adversarial strength.

CHALLENGE AND PROTEST

'Why do I have to get up in the morning?'
'Why do I have to wear a tie?'
'Why do I have to go to school?'

For many people the idea of 'thinking' has come to mean challenge, protest and argument. This is why many governments, education authorities and even parents are often against the idea of teaching thinking. They see thinking as causing endless disruption, protest and argument. This has indeed been the case where the old-fashioned notion of protest thinking has been dominant.

Yet the CoRT Thinking Program is now in use across many cultures and ideologies (Catholic, Protestant, Marxist, Islamic, Chinese etc.). This is because the CoRT Program deals with constructive thinking,

* Penguin Books, Harmondsworth, 1991

and this is rather different from the challenge and protest type of thinking. Indeed some governments see the teaching of constructive thinking as the best protection against the blanket protest thinking which is all that is usually available to mentally energetic young people who have not been taught thinking.

Challenge thinking is closely related to critical thinking and adversarial thinking. It is often felt that it is enough to protest or challenge and then the other side (or the authorities) will somehow 'make things right'. This is very much the thinking of a child demanding that its parents make things right.

There is a place for protest and much has been achieved by it: ecology concerns; moratorium on whale hunting; women's rights; minority rights; safer cars etc. Protest has its place in removing injustices and raising consciousness on an issue. Where faults can be removed, protest may be enough. In other areas which require creative and constructive thinking, protest is insufficient.

Yet there is a positive type of challenge, for without challenge we would never escape from old ideas in order to develop better ones. This positive challenge is part of creative thinking.

In the negative challenge we attack the existing idea and ask the other party to defend the idea or to improve it.

In the positive challenge we acknowledge the value of the existing idea, then we create a new idea and lay it alongside the old idea. We then seek to show that the new idea has merits and benefits.

Traditional revolutions have always been negative: define an enemy and struggle to overthrow the enemy. It is time we developed designs for positive revolutions where there are no enemies but structures for making things better.

THE NEED TO BE RIGHT

If you work out a mathematics problem and get the right answer, you stop thinking. You cannot be more right than right. But real life is not like that. You get an answer that seems 'right' but you go on thinking. You go on thinking because there are usually other answers that are better (in terms of cost, less pollution, human values, competitive advantage etc.).

Our egos become very much tied up with being right. In Western cultures that is the basis of argument and the adversarial system. We are reluctant to admit defeat because of this ego problem. The result is that our thinking is both aggressive and defensive but rarely constructive.

Theoretically everyone should be happy to lose an argument because that way you end up with more than you had at the beginning.

At meetings people want their idea to prevail – whether or not it is the best idea – because their ego is involved. Because of this serious ego problem, an important aspect of learning to think is the development of techniques to detach thinking from the ego. I shall be dealing with such techniques (like the six-hats technique) in this book.

ANALYSIS AND DESIGN

Analysis is such an important part of our thinking tradition that almost the whole of our tertiary education system (colleges and universities) is directed towards developing analytical skills.

There is no doubt that analysis is a very important part of thinking. It is through analysis that we break down complex situations into ones we can handle. It is through analysis that we find the cause of a problem and seek to remove that cause.

As with critical thinking the question is not whether analysis has a value but whether it is enough. If we now have two wheels on the motor-car, each wheel is wonderful but two wheels are still not good enough.

If you sit on a sharp object a quick analysis will allow you to remove the cause of your discomfort and to solve the problem. Many problems can be solved by finding and removing the cause. But there are also many other problems where we cannot find the cause. Or, there may be multiple interrelated causes. Or, we may find the cause (for example human greed) but are quite unable to remove the cause.

It is for this reason that we are so poor at solving such problems as drug abuse, third-world debt, pollution, traffic congestion etc. To solve such problems analysis is not sufficient. Yet all the

problem-solvers in government and elsewhere are trained in analytical thinking.

There are many problems which require 'design' as much as they
require analysis. It is with design that we construct and create
solutions. Design thinking allows us to put things together to achieve
what we desire. It is not a matter of removing the cause of the
problem but of constructing a solution.

Yet the amount of attention we give to design thinking – and creative
and constructive thinking – in education is tiny. Design is seen as
something for architects, graphic artists and fashion designers. Yet
design is a fundamental and very important part of thinking. Design
is at least as important as analysis. Design includes all those aspects
of thinking involved in putting things together to achieve an effect.

Because the traditions of Western academic thinking have been
concerned with reactive thinking, with analysis, with critical thinking, with argument and with scholarship, such fundamentally important aspects of thinking as design have been virtually neglected.

CREATIVE THINKING

In any self-organizing system there is an absolute mathematical
necessity for creativity. All the evidence suggests that the mind
behaves as a self-organizing neural network. Why have we not paid
serious attention to creative thinking when this type of thinking is
so obviously a key part of thinking (for improvement, for design,
for problem-solving, for change, for new ideas etc.)?

There are two reasons why we have neglected creative thinking. The
first reason is that we have believed that nothing can be done about
it. We have considered creative thinking to be a mystical gift that
some people have and others do not have. There is nothing that
can be done except to foster the creative gift in those who seem to
have it.

The second reason we have neglected creative thinking is very interesting indeed. Every valuable creative idea must always be logical in
hindsight (after someone has had the idea). If the new idea were not
logical in hindsight we would never be able to regard it as valuable.
So we are only able to recognize those creative ideas which are

indeed logical in hindsight. The rest remain as crazy ideas. We may catch up with some of the crazy ideas later or they may remain crazy for ever.

We then go on to assume that if the creative idea is logical in hindsight then we surely should have been able to reach the idea by the exercise of logic in the first place. So there is no need for creativity, just a need for better logic.

This assumption is totally wrong. But it is only in very recent years that we (actually a very small number of people working in this area) have come to realize that in a self-organizing information system an idea may be logical in hindsight but invisible in foresight. This arises from the asymmetric nature of patterns – which also gives rise to humour.

Because our traditional thinking systems have only dealt with externally organized information systems (moving symbols according to logic rules) we have never been able to see this point.

Those who have been advocating creativity have been equally mistaken – but in a different direction. Such people have believed that everyone is naturally creative but is inhibited. This inhibition arises from the need to provide only the 'right' answers at school. This inhibition arises from the fear of making mistakes or seeming ridiculous in business or professional life.

So if we can free people up and remove these inhibitions, we may unlock the natural creativity. This is the basis of brainstorming and similar processes for freeing people from inhibitions.

Unfortunately, creativity is not natural to the brain. The purpose of the brain is to allow experience to organize itself as patterns – and then to use these existing patterns. So freeing people to be their natural selves will only make them slightly more creative (through being less inhibited).

If we want to be more creative, then we have to develop some specific thinking techniques. These techniques form part of what I called 'lateral thinking' (which I shall describe later in the book). The techniques are unnatural and include methods of provocation which seem highly illogical. In fact such methods are perfectly logical in patterning systems.

Creativity does not have to remain a mystical gift. There are specific techniques of creative thinking and I shall be describing some of them in this book. I shall also tell how the deliberate use of these techniques of lateral thinking contributed to the saving of the Olympic Games, which nearly came to an end in 1984.

LOGIC AND PERCEPTION

Everyone knows that logic is the basis of good thinking. But is it?

Bad logic makes for bad thinking. That is clear. So good logic makes for good thinking? Unfortunately, this does not follow at all. Every junior logician knows that logic can never be any better than the starting premises or perceptions. All logicians learn this – then many of them promptly forget it.

There is a fault in your computer. Whatever you put in the output is always rubbish. The fault is put right and the computer now works flawlessly. If you put in good data you get good answers. If you put in bad data you get bad answers (though you may not know this). It is the same with logic. Like the computer, logic is a servicing mechanism to service the data and perceptions we are using. We should therefore be quick to point out bad logic but slow to accept the conclusions of good logic – because the perceptions may be inadequate.

I would say that about 85 per cent of ordinary thinking is a matter of perception. Most of the faults in thinking are faults of perception (limited view etc.) and not faults in logic. Perception is the basis of wisdom. Logic is important in technical matters and especially in closed systems like mathematics.

Because perception is so very important a part of thinking it is surprising that we persist in believing that logic is the basis of thinking. This arises from our reactive thinking habits. You put material with ready-made perceptions and information in front of students and then ask them to react. Clearly logic is important since the perceptions are provided. In real life we have to form our own perceptions.

Both logic and perception are important in the sense that both the engine and the wheels of a car are important. If I were forced to choose between the two I would have to choose perception. This is because the bulk of ordinary thinking depends on perception.

Also you can get quite far with skilful perception (as I shall explain later in the book), whereas skilled logic and poor perception can be dangerous.

In practice logic and perception are closely intertwined.

The emphasis of this book is on perception because this is the basis of wisdom and because this is the most neglected part of thinking.

EMOTIONS, FEELINGS AND INTUITION

Contrary to what many people believe, emotions, feelings and intuition play a central role in thinking.

The purpose of thinking is to so arrange the world (in our minds) that we can apply emotion effectively. In the end it is emotion that makes the choices and decisions.

The key question is when we use emotions and feelings.

There are those who feel that gut feeling is the only genuine guide to action. Such people are suspicious of logic and word games because they feel that logic can be used to prove anything (which is true if you choose your perceptions and values carefully). For such people true feeling becomes a sort of god. This is dangerous because true feeling can be both vicious and also inadequate. Much of man's inhumanity to man has been based on the true feelings of the moment.

If, however, we develop our perceptions – including alternative ways of viewing the situation – and then apply our values and feelings, the result is going to be much better.

Logic and argument cannot change feelings but perception can. A stranger you meet on holiday is very helpful. Then someone suggests he may be a con-man. Looking at the person through this new perception may lead to a change of feeling.

Instead of excluding emotion, as is normally the case with the teaching of thinking, we must find ways of allowing emotion and feeling to play their proper part in our thinking. In this book I shall describe such methods, for example the use of the 'red hat' in the six-hats technique.

Intuition does play a very important part in thinking. But it is dangerous to sit back and do no thinking on the basis that somehow intuition will work it all out for you. Intuition can be notoriously wrong sometimes – for example when dealing with probabilities. But, as with emotions and feelings, intuition has a part to play in thinking.

There are probably two major influences on young people. The first is the peer pressure of their friends, group and age bracket. This provides the perceptions and values. Unless a young person is able to think for himself or herself there is only the possibility of flowing with the group (even when this means such things as drug-taking).

The second major influence is the music of youth culture, with its repeated emphasis on the confused emotions of adolescence. Like a field of wheat waving in the breeze, young minds are subjected to hours and hours of 'he loves me – he loves me not' – with variations. Pop music is a very powerful medium and from time to time it does provide values, insights and even some thinking but, in general, the steady diet of anguished emotion does little to help individuals think for themselves.

SUMMARY

In this section I have set out to correct some of the generally held misconceptions about thinking. We need information but we also need thinking. Thinking is not just a matter of cleverness and diffi-cult problems. Wisdom is even more important than cleverness.

Traditional thinking puts all the emphasis on critical thinking, argu-ment, analysis and logic. These are very important and I hope that nothing I write gives a different impression. But these are only a part of thinking and it is very dangerous to assume they are suffi-cient. In addition to critical thinking we need thinking that is constructive and creative. In addition to argument we need explora-tion of the subject. In addition to analysis we need the skills of design. In addition to logic we need perception.

Traditionally we have been concerned mainly with reactive thinking: reacting to what is put before you. But there is a whole other side of thinking. This other side of thinking (pro-active) involves getting out and doing things and making things happen. This requires 'operacy' or the skills of doing. It requires thinking that is constructive, creative and generative.

Much of thinking has had a negative flavour: challenge, attack, criticize, argue, prove wrong etc. Is this really the only way to proceed – or can we obtain the same effects in a more constructive way? I believe we can.

Creative thinking is very important. We can begin to see how we can use creative thinking deliberately instead of just waiting for inspiration.

Emotions and feelings play a key part in thinking. It is not a matter of excluding them but of using them at the right moment.

Finally, intelligence is a potential and for that potential to be fully used we need to develop thinking skills. Without such skills the potential is under-used.

Note About the Author

Dr Edward de Bono was a Rhodes Scholar at Oxford University and has held appointments at the universities of Oxford, Cambridge, London and Harvard. He is in a unique position to write this book for the following reasons:

1. Unlike most educators Dr de Bono works not only in the field of education but also with business, government and foreign affairs. He developed the most widely used program for the direct teaching of thinking as a subject in schools (the CoRT Program). At the same time his instruction in thinking is in constant demand by the major corporations around the world, and by other bodies.

This is an important point for two reasons. The first point is that education is not a game played for its own ends. Education is a preparation for life. So the thinking skills taught in school must have a usefulness to life after school. This is not the case with many of the traditional approaches to teaching thinking. The second reason is that the world of business, government and public affairs is a tough testing ground. Students in school have to accept what is put before them. Business executives do not have to accept anything. They will accept instruction in thinking only if they believe it to be relevant, practical and important. The business world provides the ultimate test of the paying consumer.

2. More than many other educators Dr de Bono has worked throughout the world. He has worked directly in forty-five major countries (and in several small ones). His work is in use in many more. He has worked with a wide variety of cultures and ideologies. This has forced him to look at the most fundamental aspects of thinking and to free himself from thinking habits which are peculiar to just one culture. For example, this has allowed him to see clearly the limitations of Western thinking habits such as argument and critical thinking. Working with different countries, with different teachers, in far from ideal conditions has also forced him to simplify

and make very practical the teaching methods. It has not been possible to rely on inspired and highly educated teachers.

3. Unlike many people in this field, Dr de Bono is an original thinker who has tackled directly the nature of thinking and ways to teach it. Too many people in this field simply copy from others and paste together bits from here and there.

Dr de Bono's background in both psychology and medicine have put him in a unique position to understand biological 'self-organizing' information systems. This is the basis for the understanding of perception and of creative thinking. These matters will be elaborated further in the next few pages.

4. Above all, Dr de Bono's twenty-five years of experience in the field of the direct teaching of thinking as a skill put him in a very different position from those who have come lately to the field. His methods (such as the CoRT Program) have been tested over the years with a variety of ages, abilities, teachers and conditions. They have been shown to work. Even more importantly these methods have been shown to be teachable. From this large experience has come Dr de Bono's emphasis on practicality and simplicity. This was why it was possible to train 105,000 teachers in Venezuela. It is easy enough to produce complicated programs that look good but are unteachable and unusable. Since parents are not all highly qualified teachers this experience and practicality of Dr de Bono is essential for a book of this sort.

EDUCATION

Dr Edward de Bono is widely acknowledged as a pioneer in the direct teaching of thinking in schools. His first books appeared in 1967 and the CoRT Program has been in use since 1972.

He has spoken widely at education conventions (International Conference on Thinking; World Council on Gifted Children; ASCD National Convention and other meetings etc.). In 1989 he was invited to address the Education Commission of the States (USA) which brings together state governors and senior education officers from all the states. In 1989 he was invited to give the opening address to the special meeting called in Paris by the OECD to consider directly the teaching of thinking. This was a major meeting attended by all OECD countries (USA, Japan, Germany, France, UK etc.).

The CoRT Program for the teaching of thinking in schools is now widely used across Canada (including French-speaking areas). In the USA there is increasing use of the program. Minnesota, which is regarded as the lead state in education, has allocated special funds for training in this program and to set up demonstration schools.

Dr de Bono was invited to Moscow by the Soviet Academy of Sciences to train teachers in the special School Project One, which includes the leading laboratory schools in which new methods are tried out. In China the CoRT Program has been in use for some years with selected senior schools.

In Singapore the government did their own testing and then tried out the CoRT Program in forty-five schools. They are now planning to extend the program to all schools. In Malaysia the program has been in use for some years with senior schools. In Bulgaria after preliminary satisfactory tests the government is introducing the method into all schools.

In Venezuela a professor of philosophy at the university of Caracas (Dr Machado) was inspired by Dr de Bono's book *The Mechanism of Mind*. Later Dr Machado became a politician and set up a special Ministry for the Development of Intelligence. Dr de Bono was invited to Venezuela to train a core of teachers. Eventually 105,000 teachers were trained and, by law, the teaching of thinking is compulsory in all schools. Of the fourteen projects of the Ministry for the Development of Intelligence, eight were based directly on Dr de Bono's methods. A change of government was followed by the abolition of this ministry, but the de Bono program and the Family Program continue under the Ministry of Education.

The CoRT Program is also in use in various ways in many other countries: UK, Australia, New Zealand, Israel, Sweden, Kuwait, Pakistan etc.

The best research has been done by Dr John Edwards at James Cook University in Australia. For example, he showed that the use of a CoRT thinking course increased the number of students placed in the two top grades in mathematics from 25 per cent to 52 per cent.

BUSINESS

It is not surprising that business has shown more interest in Dr de Bono's work than any other part of society. In business there is a bottom line. Just defending a point of view means nothing. Thinking is concerned with actions, decisions and new ideas. This is very much what Dr de Bono is about. Business also knows that people are its main resource. That is why business has been so concerned to improve the thinking of its people.

Dr de Bono has usually been asked in at senior level to help with the thinking required for change, strategies, improvement and new directions.

The range of the corporations that have sought Dr de Bono's instruction in thinking is predictably wide, since thinking enters into all fields.

From NTT (Japan; by far the most valued corporation in the world; telephones and telecommunications) to Smurfitt (the largest company in Ireland; packaging). From IBM (computers) to Weston Group (Canada; foods). From General Motors (cars) to Dentsu (Japan; possibly the largest advertising agency in the world). From Shell (oil) to L. M. Ericsson (Sweden; radar and electronics). From Du Pont (chemicals) to Prudential (the largest insurance company). From Ciba-Geigy (Switzerland; pharmaceuticals) to McKinsey (consultants). From KLM (Holland; airline) to Citicorp (the largest US bank). From BHP (the largest Australian company in steel and mining) to Zegna (a leading Italian fashion house). From Heineken (Holland; brewing) to American Standard (bathroom fittings).

Dr de Bono is often invited to address major conferences such as: BIMCO (the world's largest shipping conference); the Institute of Institutional Investors; YPO (Young Presidents Organization); CEI (world congress of food processors) etc. etc.

PUBLIC AFFAIRS

When the US Defense Department University (Pentagon) held their first ever conference on creativity they wanted Dr de Bono to open the meeting. Since he had a prior commitment to be in

Helsinki, he opened the meeting by transatlantic telephone from Finland.

Dr de Bono has given seminars to the Los Angeles Police Department and to various other police academies and institutes.

When the American Bar Association held their first conference on conflict resolution in education they invited Dr de Bono to open the meeting. He was also invited to address the Commonwealth Law Conference, which brings together about 5,000 lawyers from all over the world.

In the field of economics Dr de Bono has been invited to speak at various meetings including the prestigious Davos World Economic Forum on several occasions, the Pacific Rim Economic Conference, the International Institute of Banking and various others.

Dr de Bono was invited by the Canadian government to give a seminar to CIDA, which is responsible for all foreign aid. The Government of California Department of Toxic Waste invited Dr de Bono to give a series of seminars and workshops to help them work out some problems with monitoring, inquiries and legislation. Various public service commissions (Australia, Canada, Singapore, Malaysia) have invited Dr de Bono to address their senior people.

Among other bodies that have sought the help of Dr de Bono have been the World Wildlife Fund and the International Union for the Conservation of Nature.

INTERNATIONAL

Dr de Bono has worked in a wide variety of countries: Canada, USA, Mexico, Brazil, Argentina, Sweden, France, UK, Germany, Italy, Spain, Egypt, Saudi Arabia, India, Pakistan, Singapore, Malaysia, USSR, China, Korea, Japan, Australia, New Zealand and in nineteen other countries, in addition to several smaller countries such as Malta, UAE, Fiji etc.

Dr de Bono's books are translated into twenty-three languages, including all major European languages, Japanese, Russian, Chinese, Korean, Hebrew, Urdu etc.

What is perhaps surprising is that Dr de Bono's work is accepted and used across widely different cultures and ideologies: Catholic, Protestant, Islamic, Marxist, Chinese, Japanese etc.

PUBLICATIONS

Dr de Bono wrote his first book in 1967. The title was *New Think*, which anticipated by twenty years Gorbachev's use of that term. Since then he has written thirty books, all of which are in the general field of thinking. The titles include: *The Mechanism of Mind*; *Lateral Thinking for Management*; *Teaching Thinking*; *Children Solve Problems*; *Practical Thinking*; *Conflicts*; *Atlas of Management Thinking*; *Six Thinking Hats*; *Letters to Thinkers*; *I Am Right – You Are Wrong*.

The BBC (London) produced a ten-part TV series called 'De Bono's Thinking Course' which was widely shown on PBS in the USA. A further thirteen-part TV series called 'The Greatest Thinkers' was sponsored by IBM (Germany) and *Encyclopaedia Britannica* and has been shown in Europe.

The CoRT Thinking Program (published by SRA) is the major educational program developed by Dr de Bono. It consists of six sections of ten lessons each. A further program that is more concerned with writing is *Think, Note, Write* (published by Perfection Learning, Iowa). Audio-cassette material called *Masterthinker* is produced by International Center for Creative Thinking (NY).

THINK ABOUT THINKING

Dr de Bono was the inventor of the term 'lateral thinking', which now has an entry, with attribution to Dr de Bono, in the *Oxford English Dictionary* and is therefore part of the English language.

Dr de Bono's background in medicine has been essential for the development of his ideas. Had he come from the fields of philosophy, mathematics or computers he would not have been able to develop his ideas, because these fields deal with externally organized information systems where symbols are manipulated according to logic rules.

In medicine, Dr de Bono did research into the integrated systems in the human body (circulation, respiration, ion control, kidney function, hormones etc.). He was therefore forced to develop biological concepts of organization and information handling. These led to concepts of self-organizing systems.

In his book *The Mechanism of Mind*, which was published in 1969, Dr de Bono described how the brain worked as a neural network which allows information to organize itself into patterns. That book was about twenty years ahead of its time, since the concepts in it now form the basis of the latest developments in computers: neurocomputers, neural net machines etc. Since its publication many more people have moved into the area of self-organizing systems and there is now a part of mathematics which deals with such matters. Various models of brain function have been put forward which, in some cases, are closely related to that put forward by Dr de Bono in 1969.

This was the basis which allowed Dr de Bono to develop his ideas on perception and on creativity. From this basis arose the techniques of lateral thinking. From this basis arose the perception-changing techniques put forward in the CoRT Program. The theoretical base for Dr de Bono's work is therefore the behaviour of self-organizing patterning systems.

More recently Dr de Bono has invited major computer and software corporations to take part in a 'Task Force on Thinking', the purpose of which is to explore the interface between the provision of information and our ability to make use of it. The first meeting of the Task Force was held in Washington DC in May 1989.

Dr de Bono is also working on the major project of creating a new international language for thinking.

EXPERIENCE

Dr de Bono has been working in the field of thinking since 1965. His first book was published in 1967 and the CoRT Program was first used in 1972. The ideas and methods have stood the test of time, practicality and usefulness.

Experience in the field of teaching thinking is important. Confusion and complexity are to be avoided at all costs because far from improving thinking they could actually make it worse.

Since the teaching of thinking has become something of a band-wagon in the USA, publishers have commissioned authors to rush out hasty and ill-prepared material. This is largely done by copying material and putting it together in a different way – which unfortunately often destroys the method. Alternatively authors have chosen to take a little bit from here and a little bit from there. The result is – as might be expected – a mess. Finally there is a re-hash of very old approaches to thinking based largely on traditional critical thinking. Many of these programs are professionally presented and nicely published. Unfortunately that is not enough. The practical experience in the field is lacking.

To analyse the thinking process into component elements and then to seek to teach these elements is not the same as designing 'practical' thinking tools.

In 1984 the Olympic Games movement nearly came to an end because no city in the world wanted the expense of hosting the Games. It was only the brilliant success of Peter Ueberroth and his team at the Los Angeles Games that showed there was a future for the Games. In an interview in the *Washington Post* Mr Ueberroth told how he had used lateral thinking to generate the new concepts that were required. He had learned the techniques of lateral thinking from Dr de Bono at a seminar some years before. This is a specific example of the practical effectiveness of Dr de Bono's thinking tools.

Mr Ron Barbaro, chief executive of the Prudential Insurance company of Canada, told how he had used Dr de Bono's thinking methods to make a major change in life insurance. Traditionally life insurance is paid out on the death of the policy-holder. The new idea was to pay out the insurance when the policy-holder was diagnosed as having a disease likely to be terminal (cancer, AIDS etc.). This would allow the policy-holder to use some of the money for better treatment and care. This has now been taken up by most insurance companies in Canada and is arousing great interest elsewhere.

SUMMARY

It is possible that Dr de Bono is the best person with the background, credentials and experience to write this book. What is so important is that he works not just in the narrow field of education but in the wide world of applied thinking. His ideas and methods have stood the test of time and paying customers.

Dr de Bono's emphasis on simplicity and practicality is essential in a subject area that is too often subjected to complexity, confusion and over-philosophizing.

Dr de Bono is concerned with the thinking involved in getting things done and in having new ideas. This goes beyond traditional reactive thinking, which is concerned only with analysis, criticism and argument.

How to Use This Book

Although this book is intended for use with children there is no upper age limit. The methods and techniques are just as suitable for adults as for children. Indeed, many of the methods have been taught to senior business executives and are used by them.

This is not surprising. The fundamental processes of mathematics are the same for every age. So are the basic thinking processes. With older children more is demanded. The techniques should be used more precisely. The answers should be more sophisticated. It becomes possible to use combinations of techniques. The practice items that are used can be more complex. Nevertheless the basic approach is the same.

The normal lower limit for most of the methods put forward in this book would be nine years old. This age limit can be lowered to about six years old with a patient parent and a simplification of the methods. It also follows that with unusually advanced children the age of use can be lower.

Following this section I shall give a list of those items in the book which are suitable for younger children. For example the drawing method can be used down to four-year-olds.

TEACHING FROM THE BOOK

There are three possible ways of teaching from the book.

1. With older, more sophisticated children and those who become interested in 'thinking', the youngster can read the whole book in parallel with the parent. The background points and the methods can be discussed. The exercises can be done together. In such cases it would be a convenience to have two copies of the book (or one for each youngster and one for the parent).

2. With younger children and those who are not motivated to go through the book, the parent should read it and digest the important information, which is then taught to the youngster. Some of the material can be skipped and some can be simplified. The parts that describe the actual processes can be read directly from the book.

3. With the youngest children and those who are least able the parent reads the book but presents only selected parts of it. If the book is treated in this abbreviated manner at one age, a fuller review of the book can be made when the youngster is older.

These three possible approaches are shown in the diagram opposite.

MOTIVATION

Motivation is the key point. Without motivation it is going to be very difficult to teach any thinking at all.

Unfortunately, telling a youngster that 'thinking' will be of great help at school or in life after school will not have a strong motivating effect with most children.

Thinking must be lively, fun, enjoyable and almost a game. My experience has shown me that children do enjoy thinking. They enjoy using their minds and having ideas. But they must be able to perform. Presenting a youngster with an almost impossible problem is the very opposite of motivation. If an exercise or practice item seems difficult or boring, move on to another item. The process is what matters, not individual items.

The period between nine and eleven years old is possibly when children enjoy thinking most of all. After that age youngsters become somewhat conservative and want only the 'right answer'. Teenagers tend to be both defensive and smug about their thinking – because of a fear of being wrong. It is always important to avoid the judgements of right and wrong. Thinking is a performance. Sometimes you perform well and at other times not so well – as is the case with all skills. You may be playing tennis at below your best but you are still playing tennis.

Much of the motivation has to come from the choice of practice items or exercises. Many of these should be fun and speculative. It is a bad mistake to focus only on heavy and serious items. The purpose of this book is to help teach thinking skills – not to provide

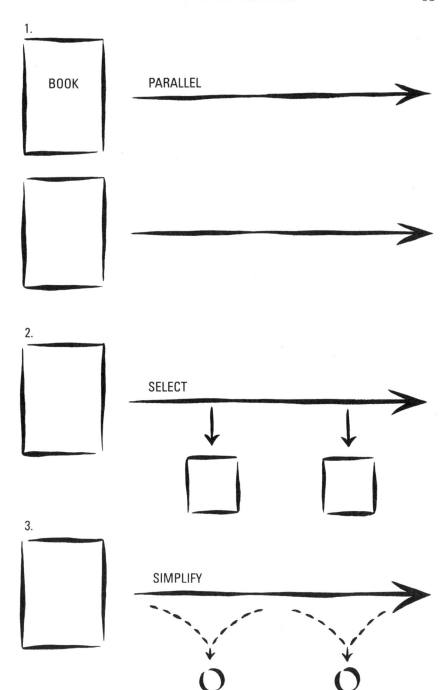

an indirect way in which parents can tell their children what they ought and ought not to do.

Motivation depends on a sense of achievement. Since there are no 'right' or single answers as such, the achievement comes in different ways. How many alternatives do you have? How does your list compare to mine? Can we add something to the list? I would never have thought of that.

There is great motivation in surprising yourself by coming up with an idea you have never had before. There is also the motivation of comparison and competition.

Finally there is the motivation of fluency. When you can ski you enjoy skiing. When you can carry out the thinking methods you enjoy doing so. Carrying out a thinking task with confidence and effectiveness is itself highly motivating.

HOBBY OR SPORT

I can see no reason why 'thinking' should not become a hobby or sport. Youngsters can meet to practise and enjoy using their minds. There is the social value, the showing-off value and the enjoyment of developing ever better skill.

The structure of the thinking methods allows thinking to go far beyond what would happen in a normal conversation or argument. These methods become the basis for developing thinking as a hobby.

The enjoyment of the skill of thinking can lead to the setting-up of 'thinking clubs'. An outline of the organization and proceedings of such clubs is given on page 302.

The thinking clubs, or just thinking sessions, could be confined to the family, to friends or to a neighbourhood group.

TEACHING STYLE

Keep it simple.

Avoid confusion.

Be very clear as to what you are doing at the moment.

Practise the method on a variety of different practice items.

The teaching style is not so very different from teaching a sporting skill or running a physical education class. As a teacher you must make clear what you want and must be sure that you have been understood. Use plenty of examples to show what you are looking for.

It is important to teach 'from the centre'. This means using very clear examples. When you come across some confusion, for example: 'Is it this or is it that?', it is best to move on to another example rather than arguing it out philosophically (which is teaching from the boundary). Always make very clear what you are trying to achieve. You may not always succeed in getting there, but at least you know what you are trying to do.

In all cases it is much better to be simple and practical than to seek to be perfect and comprehensive.

Never spend too long on any one practice item or exercise. Even if the thinking on that item is very interesting, it is important to move to another item. It is the application of the method or tool to many items which allows a person to build up skill in the use of the method. Remember always that the aim is to teach thinking skills, not just to have an interesting discussion in which some thinking is taking place.

DISCIPLINE

This is very important in the teaching of thinking skill. Without discipline there is waffle and drift and no sense of achievement.

The first discipline is that of time. The time allocated to each thinking exercise may seem very short. This is deliberate. When we first use the CoRT method in schools both teachers and students complain that they cannot possibly think about a subject in three minutes. After a while they find that they can do an amazing amount of thinking in three minutes – if they know that that is all they are going to have. The short time allowed means that the time is actually used for thinking and not for arguing and fooling around. This time discipline extends not only to each exercise but to the whole thinking session or lesson. Training in a skill always requires discipline, as any sports coach knows.

The second discipline is that of focus. What subject am I thinking about right now? What am I trying to do (method) right now? Thinking can be sloppy. A person asked to consider one problem comes up with ideas for another problem. In the course of discussion on one subject the conversation drifts to a totally different subject. While this may be the joy of 'conversation' it does not make for effective thinking.

Yet thinking should be free, unfettered and open-ended. This is true. The tighter the framework for the thinking the freer the thinking can be within that framework. A carpenter needs a strong tool and a skill in using that tool. The carpenter is free to use that tool for any purpose. But at any moment the carpenter knows what tool he or she is using and what is being done.

NECKLACE STRUCTURE OF THE BOOK

This book could have been written in a logical sequence so that the different parts followed on from each other.

This book could have been written in a tidy, organized manner so that all 'tools' were in one section and all 'structures' in another. All the 'habits' could have been in one place.

If the book had been written in such a manner it would have been impossible to use as a teaching manual.

So the order and structure in the book are specifically designed to allow you, the parent, to teach from it.

Consider a necklace (diagram opposite). Each bead is complete in itself and yet all the beads together form the necklace. In a similar way the different methods put forward in this book are usually complete in themselves. Each method can be taken away and used on its own. This approach is very different from the 'hierarchical approach' in which you cannot move on to stage two unless you have mastered stage one. Similarly stage one does not mean anything until you have got to stage two.

This necklace approach is what I sometimes call the 'parallel' approach. It means that if a teacher teaches five tools and the student does not understand one of them, is away from the class when another tool is taught, forgets a third tool and does not know when

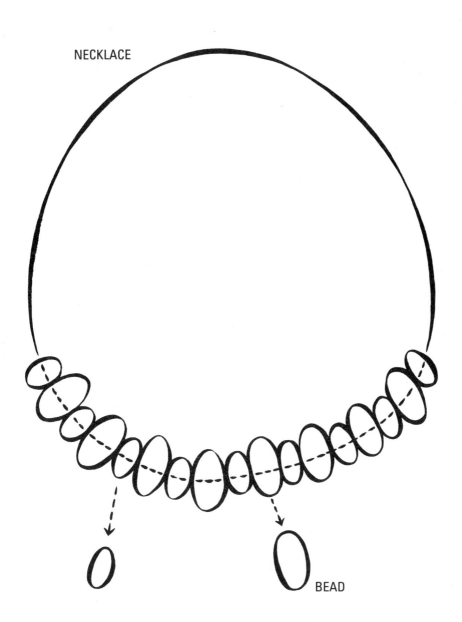

to use the fourth tool, then the fifth tool is still fully usable. It is like having several arrows in a quiver. Each one has a value on its own.

SEQUENCE

Suppose that a simple thinking procedure consists of three steps:

1. Focus

2. Use of a thinking tool

3. Outcome

Surely it would make sense to teach 'focus' first and then the 'tool' and finally how to derive an 'outcome'? This does not follow at all. The order in which the steps are going to be used is not the same as the order in which they should be taught.

There are very good reasons for teaching things 'backwards' – because you always have ahead of you something you already know – but this is not the place to go into such matters.

It makes sense to teach 'outcome' early on so that the thinker can get a sense of achievement while building up his or her skill in thinking.

The sequence used in this book is therefore a practical sequence based on many considerations – including motivation. This book is not a philosophical treatise on thinking but a practical handbook for teaching some thinking skills.

FORMAL PRACTICE

Suppose that you had never seen the game of tennis being played. You stand beside the tennis court and after fifteen minutes you feel that you have understood how the game works. Does this make you into a tennis player?

It is the same with thinking. Almost everything in this book is easy to understand. You could read through it and understand each activity or method within about five minutes. This does not make you a better thinker. It is practice that makes you a better thinker. Not just any practice of thinking but deliberate practice in the use of a tool or method. A carpenter can hold up a saw and describe how it works. But it is practice in the use of the saw that creates the skill of the carpenter.

At some point the practice does need to be formal, deliberate and disciplined. Remember also the analogy of sports training. You do have to set aside time and get down to the training.

So there is need to set aside some time for formal thinking practice. Call it a thinking 'lesson' or a thinking 'session' or some better term.

The time for the formal lesson should not be less than twenty minutes or more than forty-five minutes. Keep to the timing. These suggested timings are based on the model of one parent and one child. If there are more children, more time will be needed, so the timing could increase to a minimum of thirty minutes and a maximum of one hour.

The lesson could be held at the same time each week, or a specific day and time could be set for the next session.

Unless the motivation (on the part of the youngster, not the parent) is very high, I would suggest just one lesson a week. This could be increased to two lessons a week. If the family is on holiday, it might be possible to have one lesson a day – if the lesson is made enjoyable.

What should be covered in each session?

As a general rule no more than one new item should be covered in each session. In fact, I strongly advise that each item is spread over two sessions.

During a session, in addition to the new item, there can also be practice of items covered previously. There can also be the use of thinking games and formats. Remember always that each session must be lively and fun. Avoid getting bogged down in something tedious and boring.

INFORMAL PRACTICE

Apart from the formal practice sessions, the thinking tools, habits, methods and attitudes can be practised informally at any time.

A parent can remind a youngster of a particular thinking attitude or habit. The youngster may be asked to apply a specific tool to a situation that is already being discussed. Something may be pointed out as an example of a particular thinking method.

There are also thinking formats and games which can be introduced at any time. Each of these lasts only a few minutes.

This informal practice is very important because it is the way in which the thinking skills are integrated into normal life – instead of being a special game played only during special sessions.

It is important, however, not to overdo the informal practice to the point where it becomes irritating.

There are always two levels at which the thinking skills will be operating. The first level is the formal, explicit and deliberate use of a tool or method. For example someone might say: 'Let's do a PMI (one of the tools) here.'

The second level is the implicity or hidden level in which a habit or thinking principle is used without any formal acknowledgement. For example if someone comes to you and tells you that there are only two possible ways of doing something, you might think to yourself: 'Maybe he's right. Maybe there are only two possible ways. But I am going to spend a few seconds seeing if there might not be another way.'

Do not be shy about asking for the use of the tools and methods in a formal and explicit way. The tools are most effective when used in this explicit manner. At first it may seem awkward but in time it becomes quite natural. Do not make the mistake (which many teachers make) of believing that the attitudes and habits behind each formal thinking tool can be taught and used without actually mentioning the tool. Years of experience have shown that this is far less effective. The mind needs to have formal operations in order to direct our attention. Attitudes are good but not enough.

EXERCISES

Exercises are set at different points in this book. You should use these exercises as they are given. You may also supplement them with items of your own. But be careful not to introduce too many items which are solemn or heavy. Building up thinking skills should be fun. Once the skills are in place, they can indeed be applied to heavy matters.

There are four types of practice items:

1. FUN ITEMS: These are imaginative, crazy, speculative and not meant to be taken seriously. Although the subject matter is not serious the principles, functions and operations are quite real (as with a metaphor). 'What would happen if we all had a third arm in the middle of our chest?' 'Would it be a good idea if all children over the age of ten had to put in ten hours a week of real paid work?' 'If dogs could talk, what would change?'

2. REMOTE ITEMS: These are sensible and realistic items but fall outside the experience and needs of the youngsters who are doing the thinking exercises. They may be items from the world of business, government or adult life in general. 'What factors would you consider in choosing where to set up a new fast-food place?' 'How would you solve the problem of traffic congestion in cities?' 'What should be done with household garbage?' 'There is a lot of theft from the shop you are running, how would you solve this problem?'

3. BACKYARD ITEMS: These are items that are directly relevant to the age, peer group, local environment and interests of the youngster who is learning the thinking skills. 'Your best friend seems to be avoiding you and you do not know why – what can you do?' 'Your brother with whom you share a room keeps messing everything up – what can you do?' 'You have a choice of three things to do during the holidays – how do you make the choice?' 'How would you plan a party for your friends?'

4. HEAVY ITEMS: These are serious matters that have a direct relevance to the life of the youngster who is learning thinking. The age, interests and situation of the youngsters will influence the choice of items. New items can be introduced arising from real-life needs and difficulties. These items should be used sparingly. Above all, it is important that these serious items should not be used as an excuse for parents to 'preach' to their children. As with the other types of item, these serious items must be tackled in an objective thinking manner. 'Should young people smoke?' 'You want to have the freedom to come home late but your parents want you home early – what can you do?' 'You know that your friends are experimenting with drugs, how can you persuade them not to?' 'You can never find time to study, how can you solve this problem?' 'How can you make more friends in the neighbourhood?'

There should always be a mix of items. The fun items are important for motivation and enjoyment. These items are important for building up the skill of thinking since no emotions or prejudices or experience interferes with the thinking process. The remote items give youngsters a taste of adult thinking and real-world problems. In my experience youngsters do enjoy tackling these items. Furthermore they provide a thinking background that will become useful in later life. Thinking about such matters also makes a youngster more aware of matters in the newspapers or on television news (in fact items from the news can be used as practice items).

It is a mistake to believe that youngsters are interested only in their own backyard problems. Such items are useful in order to show how thinking can be applied to ordinary everyday matters. It is not easy to provide general items that will apply to youngsters of different ages in different environments, so parents should build up a stock of matters of direct concern to their own children.

The main purpose of the heavy items is to show that thinking skills are not just a game but can be applied to serious matters. Remember, however, that when these heavy matters are tackled there is not much practice of the thinking skill as such, since all the attention is on the content.

If I had to give a percentage of the mix of items, this would be as follows:

Stage of building up thinking skills:

40 %   Fun items
30 %   Remote items
20 %   Backyard items
10 %   Heavy items

Stage of application of skills already acquired:

20 %   Fun items
30 %   Remote items
30 %   Backyard items
20 %   Heavy items

PERFORMANCE

How are the thinking exercises/practice to be carried out?

DEMONSTRATION: You, as parent or teacher, work through a practice item in order to show how the particular method or tool should be used. You may want to prepare an item beforehand. You should also be able to tackle an item without preparation, since this is what you will be asking of your child.

JOINT: Both parent and child work through the practice item together. Each offers suggestions. As parent, you should hold back at the beginning in order to allow your child to come up with suggestions. When these seem to have run out, offer your own suggestions in order to show that these are available. Joint performance does not mean argument or even discussion – it means working together just as the cylinders in a car engine work together.

REQUEST: This is the normal teaching one-way request. You ask your child to carry out a thinking exercise. In some cases you may ask for it to be done immediately. In other cases a few minutes of thinking time is allowed. Your child can use that time to make some basic notes before responding.

PARALLEL: Here both parent and child separately carry out the thinking exercise. This is best done in note form but can even be written out. At the end of the time the two results are compared. This way of doing things can be very motivating if the youngster can see that he or she is performing almost as well as (possibly even better than) the parent. It is not suggested for less able children.

GROUP: If there is more than one child (or adult) in the role of student, the thinking exercise can be carried out as a group exercise. The parent sets the task and then the group work on it together. At the end of the allotted time the spokesperson of the group reports back.

WRITTEN: In general all the exercises can be done verbally. Notes can help. Occasionally it is useful to set a thinking task and to ask for a written output at some later time. Where the method involves the use of diagrams (as some do), the diagram is presented as the output of the exercise. In this case the output is presented during the same thinking session rather than later (instant use).

NATURE OF THIS BOOK

This book is not meant to be comprehensive and to cover all possible aspects of thinking. Nor is it meant to be a discussion of the philosophy of thinking.

The book is meant to be useful and usable.

If the book is used in a disciplined manner, there are many useful attitudes, habits, operations, tools and structures of thinking that can be taken away and used. Even if only some of these are well learned, those are still usable on their own.

Some matters that are touched upon in this book will be covered in more detail and at more depth in a later book.

Age and Ability

I shall put down here some suggestions as to how this book may be used with children of different ages and abilities. These are only suggestions, and parents are free to explore possibilities as they see fit. In my experience teachers and parents usually underestimate the ability of children to think. They also underestimate the ability of children to think about different subjects. I have often had teachers say to me: 'The students in my class are much too young to tackle that problem.' I suggest to them that they try. They try and are surprised by the youngsters' thinking ability.

SIMPLIFY

The basic rule is to 'simplify'. Rather than omitting a section entirely it is better to read through the section and then to simplify the process. It is almost impossible to over-simplify. Parts of this book are more detailed than other parts because this is only fair to older and more able children, but even these parts can be treated in a simplified manner.

Say to yourself: 'What is the simplest way I can put this across?'

Do not be afraid of leaving out something quite important. Look not at what you have left out but at what you are putting across. Simple things used effectively will make a difference to thinking skills.

Above all avoid confusion. If something seems confusing start all over again.

Ask your child to repeat back to you what you think you have been teaching. That is the best way of checking what has been understood.

Examples and practice make things clear. It is skill, not philosophy, that is being taught.

GROUPS

I shall divide potential students of this book into three broad groups:

YOUNG: Under nine years old

MIDDLE: Nine years to fourteen years

OLDER: Over fourteen years

These very rough age groupings will be altered by ability. For example a very able child in the young group may be treated as a middle-group child. A youngster of less ability in the older group may be treated as a middle-group child.

The patience of the parent will also alter the groupings. A parent who is prepared to spend time studying the book and simplifying the processes may be able to use middle-group material with a child in the young group or older-group material with a child in the middle group.

YOUNG GROUP

The 'drawing method' is very important and may be used with children as young as four or five years old. Although this method is described towards the end of this book it should be used at once.

The parent should herself or himself read Part One of this book but not attempt to teach from it.

Most of Part Two can be used directly. The model of the carpenter is a good basic model. Attitudes can be covered in a general way.

The six-hats method can be used down to the age of about six years. At this young age a simplified form would be used.

Treat the hats only in their individual use. Do not attempt to teach the 'sequence' use of the hats except with more able children.

'Outcome and Conclusion' can be taught in a simplified way but it is important. 'Forward or Parallel' can be taught in a very simplified way. 'Logic and Perception' can be omitted.

All the attention-directing tools should be attempted: CAF, APC, OPV, C&S, PMI, AGO and FIP. Experience in schools (where there are many more children per teacher) has shown that these tools can be taught down to the age of six years. They are taught in a basic form with much practice and many examples given by the parent herself or himself. There may be some problems with C&S and AGO, since children are not very good at looking at consequences or objectives.

The 'Values' section is important and should be included. The section on 'Focus and Purpose' can be omitted.

Part Three should be much simplified. The section on 'Broad and Detail' is important but difficult to teach to younger children. It is enough to get the general idea across. The 'Basic Thinking Operations' can be covered without too much detail. There is no need to go through all the thinking operations under each type of basic operation. The exercises here are useful and can be fun.

'Truth, Logic and Critical Thinking' needs to be covered since it is so important a part of thinking, but this must be done in a very simplified manner. Confusion must be avoided. 'Under What Circumstances?' is not difficult to teach and should be mentioned.

'Hypothesis, Speculation and Provocation' is quite easy to teach to younger children because this is what they do most of the time. Keep it strong and simple and do not attempt to distinguish between hypothesis, speculation and provocation.

The 'Lateral Thinking' background section can be omitted. The sections on 'Provocation and Po' and 'Movement' should be covered in a simplified manner with many examples and exercises. Children pick up these ideas from use but not from explanation.

The 'Random Word' technique works very well with children of all ages. They enjoy finding new ideas using random words. This section can be treated thoroughly – in terms of exercises.

Part Four of the book is not particularly suited to younger children. The TO/LOPOSO/GO method can be tried in a broad and general way. There are no complicated concepts here. In general the parent may have to go through the stages with the children each time. The drawing of boxes for the stages can be useful ('Fill in each box').

From the rest of Part Four I would just pick out a very simplified version of 'Arguments and Disagreements'. This would just be a matter of attempting to see what each party was thinking. The use of the attention-directing tools for 'Minor Decisions and Choices' (in that section, p. 268) could also be tried.

MIDDLE GROUP

Though the parent should read Part One there is no need to attempt to teach from it.

Part Two can be used in its entirety.

All of Part Three can be used but it may be necessary to simplify the three background sections: 'Truth, Logic and Critical Thinking', 'Hypothesis, Speculation and Provocation' and 'Lateral Thinking'.

Part Four can also be used completely, but this section is more detailed than the other sections and can therefore be simplified. It is enough to explain the basis of each section (for example as given in the review section) and to practise as many exercises as possible. Start with a strong and simple basis and then add the detail later.

Part Five can all be used.

OLDER GROUP

The whole book can be used. In fact at this age the student could have her or his own copy of the book and could read through it. For example the student should be aware of the material in Part One. It is better that the student reads through this material and then discusses this with the teacher. Such discussions should not be based on 'What is right, what is wrong, with this?' because such an attitude immediately leads the student to think that parts are good and parts are bad and weakens the development of thinking skill. The discussion attitude should be: 'What is the writer trying to put across here? How can this be useful?'

Some more able youngsters may feel that their thinking is pretty good and that they do not need Part Two because they already do all these things. Experience has shown that this is not true. People claim to do these things but do not do them. These tools have been used even with sophisticated adults and gifted children (IQ over 150). If they are so very easy, a parent can expect the youngster to use them very effectively and in detail. Understanding each tool is indeed easy – but using a tool effectively is another matter.

Part Three can be covered in detail with discussion on the background sections: 'Truth, Logic and Critical Thinking', 'Hypothesis, Speculation and Provocation' and 'Lateral Thinking'.

Part Four is particularly suited to the older group because these are complete thinking situations that they are likely to encounter. With this group all the detail can be covered.

In Part Four it is important that the discipline of going through all the steps in the structure should be insisted upon. It is very easy for older or more able youngsters to have a general feeling about a situation and to believe that this is enough thinking. The steps are not difficult to do and sometimes they may seem unnecessary. But it is important to get into the habit of going through them.

All of Part Five can be used. The newspaper exercises and 'The Ten-Minute Thinking Game' are particularly suitable for this group.

FURTHER USE AND REPEAT USE

If your children fall into the young age group parts of this book will not be immediately relevant. But those children will grow up and will pass through the middle group and the older group. Those parts of the book which were omitted the first time around can now be covered.

This book is not something that you go through once and then forget. You can go back to the book again and again. You can focus on different parts (for example the lateral-thinking techniques). You may want to re-do the section on 'Decisions and Choices' when there are many choices to be used. You may want to revise the 'Six Hats' in order to use the method as a basis for family discussions.

Thinking Behaviour

In the end there are only two sorts of thinking behaviour:

1. You want to think.

2. You have to think.

YOU WANT TO THINK: You have a way of doing something, there are no problems and you can carry on doing things in exactly the same way – but you want to see if there is a better way. Could it be done faster? Could it be done in a simpler way? Could it be done at less cost? Could it be done with less errors, wastage, pollution, danger etc.? These are the key questions that are asked in any improvement exercise. This sort of thinking is extremely important in business, in engineering, in government etc. where there is an emphasis on efficiency, effectiveness and cost cutting. The same thing applies almost as much to personal life. The difficulty is that you are not forced to do this thinking but have to want to do it.

You are making a decision or a choice. You are organizing something or laying out a plan. You are designing something. You can do all these things. You are not stuck. But you feel that if you put in more thinking then the choice, decision, organization, plan or design will be better than if you did not spend this time thinking about it. So you want to invest time in thinking things through. A thoughtful decision is likely to be better than an impulsive one. A careful design is likely to be better than the first idea that comes to mind. So you want to think. If you are aware of thinking tools and structures, you will be more motivated to think about these matters. Without such aids to thinking you may simply go over the same things again and again. In this case learning thinking skills also motivates you to use them.

We must also add that there are times when you want to think because you have come to enjoy thinking. This is when thinking has become a hobby, a sport and a skill you enjoy using.

YOU HAVE TO THINK: There is a problem you cannot solve. There is a dilemma that makes it difficult to reach a decision. There is a conflict that is growing worse. There is a need for a new idea and you cannot get one. You need to find an opportunity but cannot do so. In short you are stuck. You cannot move ahead. You have no choice. You have to think. There is no routine way of tackling the situation. Ordinary thinking will not help you. You have to think hard.

There is, of course, a distinction between your 'needs' and what we might call your 'greed'. There are times when you have to think because there is a danger or a problem that must be solved even if you are to stay where you are. If you are driving and have a flat tyre you have to solve that problem. In the 'greed' situations you want to get ahead. You want to find the money to buy a better car. You want to find a more interesting place to go on holiday. You want to set up a new business. You want to make new friends. You do not actually have to do any of these things – but you want to do them. If you want to do these things and there is no easy way of doing them then you do have to think. Even though you are yourself setting up the necessity for thinking, it is still a necessity as far as you are concerned.

It is obvious that the better you become at thinking skills the less often you will be stuck. Situations will move from the 'have to think' category to the 'want to think' category.

ROUTINE AND NON-ROUTINE

It could be said that the purpose of thinking is to abolish the need for thinking. If, through thinking, we can turn everything into a routine reaction then we do not need thinking.

To some extent we are already trying to do exactly this with our computers. We seek to set up 'expert systems' so that when the situation is presented to the computer, the computer goes through a routine of judgements and gives an answer. This should free us of the necessity to do any thinking at all. Or, it could free us to use our thinking skills in other directions.

It is quite true that from time to time we should use our thinking to question and improve existing routines – just as a golf player is always trying to improve his or her swing. In general, however, we do not need to think about routine matters.

In practice, much of our thinking behaviour is directed towards finding the right routine to use. A child goes to a doctor with a rash. The doctor has to decide whether this is measles, sunburn, allergy or some other type of rash. When the doctor has made the diagnosis, he or she can switch on the routine of treatment. In diagnosis, as in analysis, we seek to change an unknown situation into a situation in which we can use routine patterns of response. One of the main strategies in mathematics is an attempt to change a difficult problem into another sort of problem for which there is a routine procedure.

Finally there are situations where we really do need to do new thinking. These may involve new ideas, inventions, solutions to very difficult problems. The routines are not available, so simple identification of the situation is not enough. In the end our thinking will, however, consist of escaping from some routines and putting together other sub-routines in order to get a result.

There are also the routines of thinking. For example we can set up a routine of creative thinking so that in a situation that needs new ideas we can use this creative routine. At the end of this book the student will have a set of just such operational routines.

FOCUS, SITUATION AND TASK

The link between a situation that requires thinking and our ability to use our thinking skills, methods and routines is made by our ability to define the thinking need.

'The situation is that we need ten people on this trip to get the package discount. John has decided to drop out and that brings us down to nine. The task is to persuade John to come, or to find someone else, or to get John to pay anyway. Let's focus on finding someone else, first.'

I shall be dealing with focus, task and situation in detail later in the book.

In many thinking situations we only have a very general idea of the situation, focus and task. Often we do not define this or spell it out because it is assumed everyone knows the subject and purpose of the thinking.

It is, however, useful to spell out the situation, task and focus quite clearly for a number of reasons. There may be alternative views of the situation. There may be several areas of possible focus. Different thinking tasks can be set up. When things are spelled out, it is possible to carry out one task at a time.

SITUATION: What is the situation? What type of situation is it?

TASK: What are we trying to do right now? What task shall we set ourselves?

FOCUS: Where are we focusing? What are we looking at right now?

CHANGING GEARS

Many people ask me if there is an 'ideal' type of thinking that can be used for all occasions. The answer is that there is not.

A golf player has several clubs in the bag. Each club is suited to a particular purpose. You would not use the putter for driving or the driver for putting. A car with a manual gear shift has several gears which are suited to different occasions. Even on an automatic car there are forward and reverse gear shifts. You could not have something which combines both the virtues of the forward and reverse gears at the same time.

Sometimes, in thinking, we may want to behave in an opposite manner on different occasions. For example we may want to use fierce judgement to show why something cannot be done. At other times we may want to use 'movement', which is a way of moving forward from an idea (no matter how wrong the idea may be) to develop a new idea. Sometimes we want to work within the most likely framework. At other times we identify the likely framework only to escape from it.

Thinking tools and methods may at times seem contradictory. This is because each is designed for a specific purpose. A saw is designed for cutting wood. Glue is designed for sticking pieces together. These are contrary functions – but both are useful in their place.

Thinking behaviour will often require an ability to switch methods as appropriate.

PRACTICAL THINKING

We can consider three levels of practical thinking: casual, discussion, and applied.

CASUAL: The thinking that occurs in the course of daily life. Talking to people. Dealing with routine matters. Solving minor problems. Reading the newspaper or watching television. Shopping, using transport systems, setting up meetings etc.

At this level of casual thinking there would be use of the background attitudes, principles and habits of thinking that are going to be put forward in this book. There would be no need for the tools or structures. Occasionally a person might 'stop to think' and might then use a tool explicitly. In communicating with others the tools can be a useful code for getting people to think in a certain way — but they would need to know this code.

DISCUSSION: This is where people meet together for the purpose of thinking about something. There is exploration, consideration, discussion and sometimes argument.

The people know that they are at the meeting to think about the matter, to exchange ideas and feelings and to come up with new ideas.

While it is to be hoped that the attitudes, principles and habits of good thinking are available to all the people at the meeting, there is also a need for explicit and deliberate use of some of the thinking tools (for example the six-hats tool). Casual thinking is not very productive. Argument is not the best way to explore a subject.

Mostly people use no thinking structure at all at a meeting apart from an agenda and a summary. Yet if people come together for the purpose of thinking, they should use effective thinking methods. It is true that sometimes the purpose of a meeting is not thinking but communication.

APPLIED: Here there is a defined thinking need: choice, decision, plan, strategy, initiative, opportunity, problem, task, conflict etc. The situation can be defined and the thinking need can be spelled out.

It may be a matter of 'wanting to think' or of 'having to think' about the matter. General discussion will not be enough. There is a need to use some of the thinking tools and also some of the structures that can help with specific situations (for example decisions or creative needs).

AUTOMATIC AND DELIBERATE

Over time the attitudes, principles, habits and basic operations of good thinking can become automatic: they become part of the background to any thinking that is being done.

Some of the attitudes involved in the attention-directing tools can also become second-nature. The use of some of the tools may also become routine.

Nevertheless there is still a need to use some of the tools (particularly the creative thinking tools) and structures in a deliberate and disciplined manner.

Many highly creative people who have been using my techniques of lateral thinking in their professional and business lives for years tell me that they still get the best results when they set out to use the techniques in a deliberate manner: step by step.

SUMMARY

Some of the thinking skills put forward in this book will become a natural part of any thinking behaviour. Some of them will always need to be used in a deliberate and disciplined manner.

There are situations which involve thinking without the thinker making any special effort (casual thinking).

There are situations where you want to use the best thinking you can.

There are situations when you are stuck and have to use the best thinking that you can.

The Nature of Thinking

I have always regarded the humble bicycle as one of man's most remarkable inventions. This is because the bicycle is a device which allows man's own energy, muscles and bone structures to be used in a far more effective manner. On a bicycle a person can go much faster and much further. Yet no energy is brought in from outside.

Suppose we line up some people and ask them to run a race. Someone comes first, someone second and someone last. This is natural running ability. If we now design the bicycle and train people to ride the bicycles, the race would be very different. Everyone would go much faster (or further) than before.

It is the same with thinking. We can use our natural thinking ability and that will serve us quite well. But if we develop structures, methods and notations we can do very much better.

Mathematics is the perfect example. We developed notations and systems that allow us to perform prodigious feats of calculation. We did not sit back and say that natural mathematical ability was sufficient.

As with the bicycle and as with mathematics we can begin to develop methods that can make our thinking somewhat better.

THE NATURE OF MIND

On a Caribbean holiday you only have three items of clothing to put on each morning: shirt, pants and shoes. In how many ways could you get dressed?

You have three choices for what you could put on first. After you have put something on, you then have two choices. Finally there is only one item left.

So the number of possible ways you might have got dressed is actually six. The mathematics are simple: $3 \times 2 \times 1 = 6$.

If you had eleven items of clothing to put on (the more normal situation) how many choices would you have? We have eleven choices for the first item, then ten ... and so on. The mathematics are the same: $11 \times 10 \times 9 \times 8 \times 7 \times 6 \times 5 \times 4 \times 3 \times 2 \times 1 = 39,916,800$. In fact not all these choices are possible because we could not, for instance, put on our shoes before our socks. Only about 5,000 choices are feasible.

In any case, if we had to go through all these choices in order to get dressed it would take us many hours to get dressed every morning. It does not take many hours because the mind sets up routines and we just follow the routine pattern.

The mind is brilliantly designed to set up just such routine patterns for all our experience. This is because it is a self-organizing system.

SELF-ORGANIZING

Consider a chess-board. The chess player moves the pieces around the board according to the rules of the game. The pieces and the board are passive. The player provides the action. Our information systems are of this sort. We store symbols, words, figures and then move them around according to the rules of the game. The rules might be the rules of mathematics or language or logic.

Let us consider a different type of system. Rain falls on a virgin landscape. Over time the rain becomes organized into streams, tributaries and rivers. This is called a self-organizing system because the rain and the landscape together organize themselves into the pattern of water flow.

There is an increasing interest in self-organizing systems. In 1969 in my book *The Mechanism of Mind** I showed how quite simple arrangements of the nerve networks in the brain would give powerful self-organizing systems. Since then many other people have taken these ideas further. In another book, *I Am Right – You Are Wrong*,† I describe the mechanism again and show the considerable implications such an information system has for our traditional habits of thinking.

---

* Penguin Books, Harmondsworth, 1990
† Penguin Books, Harmondsworth, 1991

Our understanding of perception, of humour and of creativity depends directly on an understanding of self-organizing systems. Humour is actually the most significant behaviour of the human mind – because it identifies the type of system. That philosophers and psychologists have traditionally neglected humour and creativity shows that they have only been looking at passive systems, not self-organizing systems.

Self-organizing systems set up patterns. Once we are on a pattern we have no choice but to flow along that pattern. The patterns are fixed for a set of circumstances, but if the circumstance changes the patterns can be different. So the true model is not a fixed landscape but several alternative landscapes.

WHAT CAN WE DO?

If the brain sets up patterns, what can we do? Do we not just have to follow the patterns?

Imagine a slope (diagram opposite). You place a ball at the top of the slope and the ball rolls down the slope. The ball is rolling down the slope on its own – but you have chosen to place the ball at the top of the slope.

Imagine that the slope is quite wide and at the bottom there is a matchbox. Your task is to knock the matchbox over. You cannot just place the ball anywhere at the top of the slope. You choose a position such that the rolling ball will hit the matchbox.

In exactly the same way, thinking is a combination of what the mind does and what we set it up to do.

Add up the numbers $5 + 11 + 16$. That is easy enough. Some people might find it easier if the numbers were arranged one under the other (diagram on p. 60). Some very young people might find it easier if they were put down as dots in a row and then you just count all the dots. In this example we see how we can arrange things so that the mind finds it easier to work.

If you are asked to tell which of two similiar square shapes is the bigger you might have a hard job estimating the difference. But if you are able to place one square over the other, you can instantly see which is the bigger. Again we have re-arranged things to make the mind's task easier.

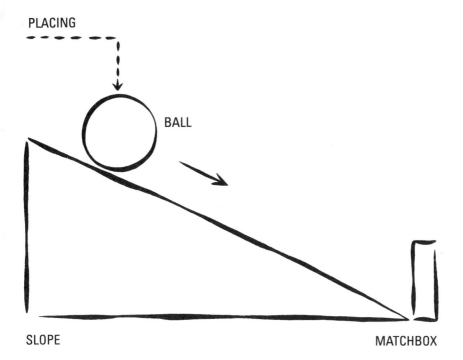

PLACING

BALL

SLOPE

MATCHBOX

$$5 + 11 + 16$$

$$
\begin{array}{r}
5 \\
11 \\
16 \\
\hline
\end{array}
$$

• • • • •   • • • • • • • • • • •   • • • • • • • • • • • • • •

5   11   16

You are sitting in a sports stadium (tennis, baseball, football) surrounded by thousands of people. You say to yourself: 'I want to pick out all those people wearing yellow clothes.' You now look around the stadium and you will see that people wearing yellow clothes seem to 'jump' out of the crowd. You have prepared your mind to see 'yellow'. You have drawn attention to yellow.

ATTENTION-DIRECTING TOOLS

Many of the tools of thinking are simply attention-directing tools. Perception is a matter of directing attention instead of just letting it flow where it will.

Sometimes the tools or structures allow us to do one thing at a time instead of doing everything at once.

Sometimes the structures are there so that we can do things in the most effective sequence. In a way that is the purpose of notation in mathematics.

So even though the mind has its own characteristics we can do things that allow those characteristics to work in our favour.

There is no contradiction between the natural behaviour of the mind and the idea of deliberate thinking.

TRAINING

The purpose of training for an athlete or a sportsperson is to eliminate mistakes and to build up the most useful routines of performance. In this case the performance is of the muscles activated by their nerves.

Some of the training in thinking is of this sort. We may try to eliminate errors or at least to label errors so that if they occur they can be recognized. We try to build up useful routines (for example the willingness to look for alternatives).

SUMMARY

As a self-organizing system the mind allows incoming information to organize itself into routine patterns. The mind, therefore, has a natural behaviour of its own. We can, however, intervene so that this natural behaviour is used more effectively for our purposes. We can develop attention-directing tools and structures. In addition, through training, we can try to set up routine patterns that are more effective than the natural ones. All these things form the basis for the development of thinking skills.

PART TWO

Carpenters and Thinkers

My favourite model for a thinker is that of the carpenter. Carpenters do things. Carpenters make things. Carpenters do things step by step. Carpenters deal with the physical substance of wood – so we can see what they are doing.

BASIC OPERATIONS

The basic operations of a carpenter are few and we could summarize them as three:

1. Cutting

2. Sticking

3. Shaping

Cutting means separating out the piece you want from the rest. As I shall explain later this corresponds to the thinking operations of: extraction, analysis, focus, attention etc.

Sticking means putting things together with glue or nails or screws. The corresponding thinking operations include: connections, linkages, synthesis, grouping, design etc.

Shaping means setting out to achieve a certain shape and comparing what you have at the moment to what you want. In thinking this corresponds to: judging, comparing, checking and matching.

So the basic operations of a carpenter are quite few (actually there are some others like drilling and polishing) but with these few operations a carpenter can make complicated objects.

TOOLS

In practice the carpenter uses tools to carry out the basic operations. The carpenter does not just say, 'I want to cut this,' but picks up a saw and uses the saw. These tools have been developed over the centuries as effective ways of carrying out the basic operations.

So we have saws, chisels and drills for cutting.

So we have glue, hammer and nails, screws and screwdriver for sticking things together.

So we have planes and templates for shaping things.

In exactly the same way we can have tools for thinking. Some of these tools (like the PMI) will be presented in this book.

The carpenter builds up skill in the use of the tools. Once the carpenter has acquired the skilful use of the tools, they can be used in different combinations to do different things.

A saw is something quite definite. In the same way the thinking 'tools' are also definite and need to be treated in this manner. When you use a saw you use a saw and not just a 'method of cutting'.

STRUCTURES

There are times when the carpenter needs to hold things in a certain position so that he or she can work upon them. For example you need to hold the wood steady in order to saw through it. You need to hold the wood steady so you can drill the holes where you want them. For this purpose there are vices and work-benches.

When the carpenter wishes to glue certain pieces together he puts the pieces in a sort of holding structure called a jig. This is a supporting structure which enables him to carry out his construction.

In exactly the same way there are thinking 'structures' that will be presented in this book. These are ways of holding things so that we can more easily work on them.

ATTITUDES

A carpenter usually has some background attitudes towards his or her work.

The attitude may be one of always seeking simplicity.

Another attitude may be an emphasis on durability.

Strength is a background attitude for all carpenters.

In the same way a good thinker has certain background attitudes which are always present in his or her thinking.

PRINCIPLES

Attitudes are more general and principles are more specific. Often the two overlap.

A carpenter will also build up a number of guiding principles of things to do and things to avoid.

These principles might include:

Go with the grain of the wood.

Arrange the maximum sticking surface for all joints.

Measure everything.

Use a thin layer of glue.

In the same way there are certain basic principles which guide thinking. For example, good thinking will always want to examine the specific circumstances in which a statement is true.

HABITS

A carpenter develops certain work habits. These may not come naturally and the carpenter may have to keep reminding himself or herself of the habit until it does become automatic.

Such habits may include:

Always replacing a tool in the rack immediately after use.

Regular sharpening of the cutting edges.

Frequent checking of a shape against the template.

Sometimes the habit may consist of the automatic application of a principle, so the distinction between the two may not always be clear. The important point is that habits are routine procedures.

In the same way there are routine habits which a good thinker seeks to build up. For example, as a matter of routine, a good thinker will always pause to see if there are alternatives at any point. There may be alternative ways of looking at the situation, alternative explanations, alternative courses of action, alternative values etc.

SUMMARY

So the model of the carpenter provides us with all the elements of thinking skill that I shall be describing in this book.

ATTITUDES: The attitudes with which we approach thinking.

PRINCIPLES: The guiding principles that make for good thinking.

HABITS: The routines we seek to make automatic.

BASIC OPERATIONS: The fundamental operations of thinking.

TOOLS: The thinking tools we practise and use deliberately.

STRUCTURES: Formats in which we hold things for convenience.

Always keep in mind the model of the carpenter as he or she goes about constructing things.

Attitudes

Attitudes affect our whole approach to thinking, so I shall begin here with looking at the attitudes of the good thinker. These should then become the attitudes with which the rest of the book is approached.

Habits and principles will be dealt with later on in the book – after there has been a good deal of thinking practice. That is the best time to summarize the principles and habits.

BAD ATTITUDES

It will be easier to appreciate the right attitudes towards thinking if we look first at some of the bad attitudes.

. . . 'Thinking is not important. Gut feeling is all that matters.'

. . . 'Thinking is boring and confusing and never gets anywhere.'

. . . 'I find all problems too difficult.'

. . . 'Thinking is only for academics and intellectuals – other people have to get on with things without thinking about them.'

These are all negative or defeatist attitudes from people who have no confidence in their thinking and have not been taught to think. But there is also the opposite type of bad attitudes when people are too arrogant about their thinking and have a wrong view of the purpose of thinking.

. . . 'I find thinking very easy. You just look at something and make up your mind about it.'

. . . 'I find that I am always right. I have no trouble defending my ideas.'

. . . 'The main purpose of thinking is to prove that those who disagree with you are wrong.'

... 'If you never make mistakes in your thinking then you must be right.'

... 'There is one right answer and anyone who cannot see it must be stupid.'

Some of the above attitudes may seem extreme and people would rarely put them into words. But if you observe the thinking of many people you would come to the conclusion that their thinking is indeed based on such attitudes.

GOOD ATTITUDES

These are the attitudes I would expect to find in a good thinker. Many good thinkers already use these attitudes, having developed them as part of their natural 'wisdom'. If you already have such attitudes it is useful to see them spelled out and confirmed. If you do not already have such attitudes it can be useful to acquire them.

First of all there are attitudes towards the skill of thinking itself.

... 'Everyone has to think – everyone can think.'
Thinking is not only for very clever people or people in specialized areas. Everyone uses thinking at different times. Everyone can develop a useful skill in thinking.

... 'Thinking is a skill that can be developed.'
Thinking is not like your height or the colour of your eyes – about which you can do nothing. Thinking is a skill like skiing, swimming or riding a bicycle. The skill of thinking can be acquired.

... 'I am a thinker.'
This is the best attitude of all. It does not matter how good a thinker you may be. It is enough that you consider yourself a thinker.

... 'I can get better and better at thinking.'
This is important. Even the best thinker can get better and better. From this attitude arises the effort to improve thinking skill all the time.

... 'Thinking may require a deliberate effort.'
It is not enough to suppose that being a good thinker is enough and that therefore all thinking will be good. There are times when thinking requires a deliberate effort – perhaps the use of a tool or structure. Thinking is not always automatic.

... 'Things that appear complicated at first can often be made more simple.'

Do not be put off by apparently complicated matters. Be ready to tackle them. It may be possible to make them more simple – if not, there is no harm in having tried.

... 'Take one step at a time.'

If you take one step at a time and keep going, you can tackle most things. Know what step you want to take and take it.

... 'Separate your ego from your thinking. Look at your thinking objectively.'

This is very difficult to do but necessary if you want to become a good thinker. 'You' and 'your thinking' are two separate matters.

... 'The purpose of thinking is not to be right all the time.'

The purpose of thinking is to get better ideas and to get better at thinking. If you have to be 'right' all the time, you only end up where you started.

... 'Listening and learning is a key part of thinking.'

Thinking is not only what you are putting forward but also what other people are putting forward.

... 'Always be humble – arrogance is the mark of a poor thinker.'

It is not always easy to be humble when the people around you are prejudiced, blind, limited in their view and plainly wrong. But you should make the effort within your own thinking. Consider that your own thinking may be wrong or incomplete or only one view of things.

Those were some attitudes towards the skill of thinking and its use. Now we can consider some attitudes about the nature of your thinking.

... 'Thinking should be constructive, not negative.'

It is not enough to attack and to prove the other party wrong. This negative type of thinking is far too common. There are times when it has a value, but that value is very limited. Start out trying to be constructive and to take things further.

... 'Explore a subject instead of arguing about it.'

If the purpose of argument is really to explore the subject, then you can jointly explore the subject much more effectively by choosing to explore it rather than to argue.

. . . 'The other party in an argument usually has something useful and constructive to say, if you make the effort to pick this out.'
Instead of just looking for points of attack, try to see what is of value in an opposing position.

. . . 'People with differing points of view are usually right according to their own special perception.'
Instead of considering others stupid try to see their perception and why they hold the view they hold.

. . . 'It is possible to be creative and to have new ideas.'
Creativity is not a special gift which only some people have. You can make an effort to have new ideas (you can also use some specific techniques to help you).

. . . 'Do not be afraid to try out ideas.'
You do not have to be right all the time. You can try out tentative ideas. You can even use deliberate provocations – provided you indicate they are intended as provocations.

. . . 'At any point in thinking there may be alternatives that you have not yet thought of.'
Never believe that your thinking has covered all possible alternatives. Although this may occasionally be true, there are very often alternatives – even obvious ones – that you have not yet thought of.

. . . 'Avoid dogmatism even when you do feel that you are right.'
If your idea is good enough, it does not need the dogmatism. If your idea is not good enough, the dogmatism is misplaced. You can always say. 'From the information I have, it seems to me that . . .'

This list of attitudes is not exhaustive. You can probably add to the list. The attitudes listed can be expressed in many different ways. Some things that might have been put down as attitudes (such as 'Think slowly' or 'Always consider the values involved') I have put down under principles or habits. There can be a lot of overlap in such matters. Under 'attitudes' I have tried to include only the general approach to thinking rather than specific guidelines.

EXERCISES FOR ATTITUDES

1. Explain and discuss the notion of 'attitudes'. This could include attitudes to sport, to music, to friends, to school etc.

2. Read through the list of bad attitudes. Do you think any of your friends have these attitudes? Discuss why some people might have these attitudes. Discuss why these might be bad attitudes.

3. See if you can add any further bad attitudes to the list. You may even do this by breaking down a listed bad attitude into more parts.

4. Go through the good attitudes, one by one, and discuss why the attitude is a good attitude. You may be able to suggest specific circumstances in which the attitude is not so good – but avoid doing this for fear of creating confusion. It is enough if the attitude, by and large, is a useful attitude.

5. Set as a task the picking-out of the five most useful of the attitudes. The purpose of this task is not really to select the most useful five but to get an examination of all the attitudes (which is necessary for the selection process).

6. If you have to combine the good attitudes to a smaller number how would you do it? (This exercise is suitable for older or more able children.)

7. If you had to add to the list of good attitudes what might you add? (This can be done on a discussion basis or set as a written task.)

(NOTE: In all these exercises the request is usually directed to the child or student – as if the exercises were to be placed in front of the child.)

The Six Thinking Hats

Have you ever tried: balancing a big book on the top of your head, juggling with two balls with your left hand and unwrapping a chocolate bar with your right hand? It would probably be rather difficult. Doing a lot of different things at the same time is always difficult and confusing.

In our thinking we often try to do too much at the same time. We look at the facts of the matter; we try to build up a logical argument; our emotions come in somewhere; we may try to put in a new idea; we try to see whether our idea will work. We do all this more or less at the same time. It is no wonder that we sometimes get confused. At other times we may do only one of these many things well – for example our emotions may dominate our thinking or we may just be very negative.

The six thinking hats is a method for doing one sort of thinking at a time. Instead of trying to do everything at once we 'wear' only one hat at a time. There are six coloured hats and each colour represents a type of thinking.

WHITE HAT: Facts, figures and information. What information do we have? What information do we need to get?

RED HAT: Emotions, feelings, hunches and intuition. What do I feel about this matter right now?

BLACK HAT: Caution. Truth, judgement, fitting the facts. Does this fit the facts? Will it work? Is it safe? Can it be done?

YELLOW HAT: Advantages, benefits, savings. Why it can be done. Why there are benefits. Why it is a good thing to do.

GREEN HAT: Exploration, proposals, suggestions, new ideas. Alternatives for action. What can we do here? Are there some different ideas?

BLUE HAT: Thinking about thinking. Control of the thinking process.

Summary of where we are now. Setting the next thinking step. Setting the program for thinking.

Each of the hats will be covered in much more detail in the next pages.

If you look at a large-screen projection television you will see that each of the three tubes gives out a different colour. On the screen all colours come together to give full-colour pictures. The same is true of ordinary television sets except that we cannot see the separate colours. The same is true of colour photography, where the different basic colours are treated separately but then come together to give full colour. Full-colour printing on paper is the same. Each of the basic colours is printed separately (colour separation) but the different colours come together to give full colour. It is exactly the same with six-hat thinking. The colours are treated separately so that we can make a good job of each colour. Then the colours come together to give us full-colour thinking.

There is some evidence that the chemicals in the brain might be slightly different when we are being creative or positive or negative. If this is so then we have to separate the different types of thinking, because we cannot at any one moment have the best setting for different types of thinking.

WHY HATS?

We often say: 'Put on your thinking cap.' There is a traditional association between caps/hats and thinking.

Hats often define a role we are playing at the moment: a baseball cap, a soldier's helmet, a nurse's cap etc.

Most important of all, hats can easily be put on and taken off. A hat is not permanently attached to you. A hat is the easiest item of clothing to put on or take off. This point is important because every person must be able to put on or take off each of the hats.

The hats are not categories. It is quite wrong to say: 'She is a green-hat thinker,' or 'He is a black-hat thinker.' The purpose of the hats is exactly the opposite of this. Instead of labelling people and putting them into boxes the hats are there to encourage people to use all types of thinking.

ROLE-PLAYING

... 'Let's have four minutes green-hat thinking on this.'

... 'What are the facts? Some white-hat thinking, please.'

... 'Be realistic. Put on your black hat.'

... 'Switch from the black hat to the yellow hat for the moment.'

When a person puts on a hat he or she plays the role that belongs to the hat. This becomes a sort of game.

If you do not think the idea will work but someone asks you for some 'yellow-hat thinking', you make an effort to find positive points about the idea.

If at a meeting someone asks for three minutes of 'green-hat thinking', all those present make an effort to come up with alternatives and new ideas.

You can choose to put on your red hat and say: 'Wearing my red hat this is what I feel about this situation – it stinks.'

This role-playing serves to detach the ego from the thinking.

The thinker is now carrying out a performance (a green-hat performance, a black-hat performance, a yellow-hat performance). The thinker shows his or her skill and gets a sense of achievement from carrying out that performance well.

This role-playing frees thinkers. Even if you like an idea, you are free to come up with black-hat ideas of why it may not work. Putting on the green hat frees you to suggest new ideas. Putting on the red hat frees you to express your hunches and feelings – without any need to justify them.

At the same time as the six-hats system frees thinkers it is also a way of forcing thinkers to think more broadly. Asking someone to put on the green hat is a specific request for that person to try to be creative. Asking a group for black-hat thinking is a request for them to assess the idea very carefully.

USE OF THE HATS

1. YOURSELF: You can choose to put on a hat in order to tell others the sort of thinking you are going to do.

... 'Putting on my black hat I am going to point out what is wrong with the idea ...'

... 'I am going to put on my red hat because I have a hunch this is all a trick. I do not know why but that is my hunch.'

... 'Putting on my green hat I want to put forward a new idea. Why don't we let people buy their motor-cycles from us?'

... 'I want to do some yellow-hat thinking here. There are the following good points about the idea ...'

... 'We do not seem to be getting anywhere. Putting on my blue hat I suggest we make clear what we are trying to do.'

You can also give yourself instructions to put on one or other hat when you are working out something on your own. You may even put down a sequence of hats and then work through them.

2. SOMEONE ELSE: When talking to someone else you can ask that person to put on a particular hat, to take off a particular hat or to switch hats. This allows you to request a change in thinking – without offending the other person.

... 'Please give me your black-hat thinking on this matter. We do not want to make any mistake.'

... 'Never mind what we can do. I just want some white-hat thinking. What are the facts?'

... 'That is what you feel about it. Now take off your red hat.'

... 'I am going to ask you to switch from black-hat thinking to some yellow-hat thinking.'

... 'What about some new ideas? Can we have some green-hat thinking on this matter?'

3. GROUP: When working with a group the leader of the group, or anyone else, can ask individuals in the group – or the whole group –

to put on, take off, or switch hats. This use is similar to use with one other person – except that more people are involved.

... 'Let's all try three minutes of green-hat thinking.'

... 'I want to know what you all really feel about this project – so some red-hat thinking from each one of you.'

... 'I think we need some white-hat thinking here. Do you all agree?'

... 'Some blue-hat thinking, please. Suggestions on the direction our thinking should take.'

THE SIX THINKING HATS IN USE

In December 1986 I gave a short talk on the six-hats method at a hotel in Tokyo to a meeting of senior Japanese executives. The occasion was the publication of the Japanese edition of my book on the subject. At that meeting there was present the chief executive of NTT (Mr Hisashi Shinto). NTT (Nippon Telephone and Telegraph) employed 350,000 people at that time. At the time of writing this book NTT is by far the most highly valued corporation in the world (stock market valuation). In fact if all four top US corporations are put together their value would be less than that of NTT.

Mr Shinto was delighted with the method and bought hundreds of copies of the book, which he asked his executives to read. Later he told me that the method had had a powerful effect on the thinking of his people, so much so that he invited me back to talk to the board and all senior management. Many other corporations around the world are now introducing the method as part of the corporate culture.

When everyone comes to understand the hats, meetings become much more productive, because instead of endless argument there can be disciplined exploration of a subject.

The six-hats method works just as well with children as with adults. The method can be used as a framework for family discussions.

ATTENTION DIRECTING

The six-hats method is really an attention-directing tool, because it directs our attention towards certain aspects and towards a certain type of thinking. For example the red hat allows us to pay attention to our feelings.

EXERCISES ON THE SIX THINKING HATS (GENERAL)

1. Discuss the method in general terms and in particular the role-playing aspect.

2. In what sort of situations do you think the six-hats method would be most useful? Give examples of thinking situations where you, yourself, might like to use one or other of the hats.

3. Do you think the six-hats method would be easy to use in practice? What would the difficulties be? Why might some people object to the use of the hats?

4. The number of hats is kept down to six for the sake of convenience. But if you had to suggest further hats what type of thinking might these further hats cover? (Suitable for older or more able children.)

5. For each of the following remarks, indicate what hat you think the speaker was wearing at the time:

'This car can accelerate at 60 mph in just 6 seconds. The fuel consumption is 25 miles per gallon in traffic.'

'Why don't we sell the factory and then lease it back?'

'At this point we should list the options we have.'

'I don't like him and I don't want to work with him.'

'I don't think that putting up the price of gasoline will make people drive more carefully.'

'If I don't get asked to his birthday party then I don't have to spend money buying a present.'

'It is not possible to climb over that wall.'

White-Hat Thinking and Red-Hat Thinking

I shall be taking the six hats two at a time because this makes it easier to learn the use of the hats and to carry out exercises with them.

WHITE HAT

Think of blank paper. Think of a computer print-out. The white hat means neutral information. It is not a matter of argument or making suggestions. White-hat thinking focuses directly on the available information.

Information is very important for thinking, so it is useful to have a way of being able to focus directly on information.

Under the white hat there are three key questions:

1. What information do we have?

2. What information is missing?

3. How do we get the information we need?

The Information We Have:

We lay out all the information we have.

The information may be facts, figures, lists, statistics etc.

The information may be our own personal knowledge or experience. In this case it must be labelled as such: 'In my experience ...'; 'As far as I know ...'

In addition to the obvious information we also read between the lines to see what other information is actually available. Every good detective in fiction picks up clues which other people have not noticed.

There are different levels of the truth, probability or solidity of the information. There are also guesses and deductions and possibilities. The important thing in white-hat thinking is to state clearly what type of information it is:

... 'This is a fact as shown in these tables.'

... 'My guess is that ...'

... 'From the way the keys have been left in the car I deduce the driver must have intended to return.'

... 'The generally accepted view is that the greenhouse effect will get serious in fifty years' time.'

Missing Information:

We examine the information we have in order to see what is missing. We try to find the gaps in our information. Do we have enough information for our thinking or for our decision? If we do not have enough information what else do we need?

Try to define the information needs as clearly as possible. It is always nice to have as much information as possible, but what do we really need?

We may need information in order to chose between two possible explanations. We may need information in order to select the best course of action. We may need information about a material to know if it will serve our needs.

Getting the Information We Need:

Listening is part of white-hat thinking. We listen carefully and pick up information – not only what is intended.

We get information by reading or by knowing how to consult computers and databanks.

The most useful way of getting information is by asking questions. Knowing the right questions to ask is a very important part of thinking. What do you want the question to do for you? Do you want to check something? This is a shooting question, since we know what we are aiming at – and the answer is a 'yes' or 'no'. Or are we fishing for information – not knowing what we will catch (fishing question)?

Under the white hat we may also be asked to say how we intend to get the missing information. It might be through information search, it might be through direct research, it might be through conducting an opinion poll etc.

Information and Feeling:

There are times when the white hat and the red hat can get quite close. When we are looking forward into the future we can never be certain, so we are guessing or extrapolating. You might say: 'I have a feeling this toy will sell.' Obviously you cannot be certain. If, however, you can provide good reasons (sales of similar toys, test markets etc.) it is white-hat thinking. If you can provide no reasons, it is red-hat thinking. As far as possible white-hat thinking should stick to information that can be checked or has some reasonable basis.

If you say: 'Mr Herring does not like this idea,' that is white-hat thinking because you are reporting a fact. If, however, you say: 'I don't like this idea,' that is your feeling and so is red-hat thinking. Even if there are good reasons for your feeling it is still red-hat thinking.

Challenge:

If someone puts forward information as being correct and someone else challenges it as being incorrect, what happens? Quite simply both views are put down, alongside each other.

... 'Mr Jones has said that the number of road deaths per year in the USA is 50,000. Mr Klein disagrees and states that the number is 70,000. We had better have those figures checked.'

RED HAT

Think of fire and warm. The red hat is for emotions, feelings, hunches and intuition.

In a way the red hat is the opposite of the white hat. The white hat seeks to put down the objective facts and is not interested in what anyone feels about them – facts are facts. The red hat is not interested in the facts but only in people's feelings.

Feelings are a very important part of thinking. Feelings come into thinking all the time. We seek to be objective but (outside of mathematics) are rarely objective. In the end all choices or decisions are based on feelings. I shall be dealing with feelings again later in this book and in more detail.

The purpose of the red hat is to allow us a way of putting forward our feelings so that they can take part in the thinking. Feelings are valuable so long as we label them as feelings. The problem arises if we pretend feelings are something else. The red hat provides a clear label.

Intuition is often based on experience about a matter. We have an 'intuition' that something is the right thing to do. But we cannot exactly explain how we reached that conclusion. Often intuitions are very valuable. Occasionally, intuitions are disastrous (in matters of probability).

Justification:

Normally, when we put forward a hunch or an intuition we seek to construct a reasonable basis for the hunch or intuition. Often this basis is false (and can be shown to be false), while the intuition or hunch has a validity.

The red hat allows the thinker to put forward a hunch or intuition without any need to support or justify it.

... 'Putting on my red hat I have this hunch that he is going to turn out to be a great tennis player – don't ask me why.'

In fact there should never be any attempt to support or justify red-hat thinking. Such support destroys the whole purpose of the red hat. The red hat is permission to put forward feelings, hunches and intuitions simply because they are there – not because they are justified.

At This Moment:

The red hat covers feelings 'at this moment'. At the beginning of a meeting a person's red-hat feelings may be quite different from what they will be at the end of the meeting.

A feeling is only valid if it is genuine and sincere. That means the feelings of the moment. A thinker may choose to refer to feelings at other times but must make this clear.

... 'My usual feelings on this purchase of a motor-bike is that it is very dangerous – but right now I feel that it might be a good idea.'

Mixed Feelings:

It is perfectly possible to have mixed feelings – and they should be reported as such.

... 'There are some aspects I feel good about – and others I feel bad about.'

You then spell out the different aspects and the feelings for each. Nevertheless, if a conclusion is required (for example in making a decision), the thinker may need to have an overall feeling.

... 'I like this and I don't like that – but on balance I like the idea.'

SUMMARY

White-hat thinking is to do with information.

Red-hat thinking is to do with feelings.

EXERCISES ON WHITE-HAT AND RED-HAT THINKING

1. What is the difference between white-hat and red-hat thinking?

2. Can computers do red-hat thinking?

3. A boy has kicked a ball into a neighbour's yard and has broken a window. They are yelling at each other. Give three examples of red-hat remarks for each side.

4. Do some white-hat thinking on the road or street in which you live.

5. Someone suggests to you that you should take up one of three hobbies: gardening, carpentry, stamp collecting. Do some white-hat thinking on each. Then follow this with red-hat thinking on each.

6. Which of the following are white-hat thinking and which are red-hat thinking?
'Pollution is a growing problem.'
'I feel pollution is now the world's number one problem.'

'We are not doing enough to control pollution.'
'Pollution is everyone's business.'
'Household garbage contributes to pollution.'
'Polls show that people do care about pollution.'
'I do not know what I can do about pollution.'

7. For a young person about to choose a career what aspects would be covered by white-hat thinking and what aspects would be covered by red-hat thinking?

8. In choosing a colour with which to paint the walls of your room, what aspects are white-hat thinking and what aspects are red-hat thinking?

9. Put on your red hat and list three things you really like and three things you do not like.

Black-Hat Thinking and Yellow-Hat Thinking

Both the black hat and the yellow hat are forms of judgement. With the black hat we are concerned with truth and fit. With the yellow hat we are concerned with benefits. Both hats have to be entirely logical. With both hats there have to be strong reasons for what you say. If there are no reasons, you should be using the red hat, because a statement without reasons is a feeling or intuition.

BLACK HAT

Think of a stern judge. Think of someone who gives you a black mark if you get something wrong.

The black hat is certainly the most used of all the hats. In some ways it is also the most valuable of the hats. The black hat prevents us from making mistakes and doing silly things.

The black hat is concerned with truth and reality. The black hat is the hat of critical thinking: 'Is this right?'

Under the black hat come a number of questions:

1. Is it true?

2. Does it fit?

3. Will it work?

4. What are the dangers and problems?

Is It True?

The black hat judges the truth of a statement or claim. Is it true or false? Does it fit the facts?

The black hat also judges the validity of a line of reasoning. Does your conclusion follow from your evidence? Have you made a mistake? Is your claim justified?

The black hat searches for what is true and correct by pointing out errors.

Does It Fit?

Does this suggestions fit in with our experience?

Does this suggestion fit in with the system in which we are working? The system includes the procedures of the organization, the law, the rules, the social customs etc.

Does this suggestion fit in with our objectives, our plans or our policy?

Does this suggestion fit in with our values, our ethics and what we consider to be fair and just?

Because the black hat is always a logical hat, you must always give the reasons why something does not seem to fit.

Will It Work?

Will the idea work?

Will the invention or machine work?

Will the plan work?

If, wearing the black hat, you say that something will not work, you must give the reasons why you say this. If you just have a 'feeling' that it will not work then that is the red hat.

What are the weaknesses in the idea?

What are the Dangers and Problems?

If we were to go ahead with this suggestion what are the dangers?

If we were to go ahead with this suggestion what problems might arise?

If we were to go ahead with this suggestion what are the likely harmful effects?

These are the questions the black-hat thinker asks himself or herself when looking at a suggestion.

Over-Use:

It is quite true that the black hat can be over-used. There are some people who want to be cautious and negative all the time. They are always ready to point out why something will not work or cannot be done.

This does not mean that the black hat is a 'bad hat'. Some salt on food is good, too much salt is bad. Food itself is good and essential for life – but too much eating makes us fat and unhealthy. Over-use of salt and food does not make salt and food bad. Over-use of the black hat does not make it a bad hat.

The black hat is a very important and very powerful hat. It would be difficult to do anything without the help of the black hat.

YELLOW HAT

Think of sunshine and optimism. The yellow hat is full of hope – but as it is a logical hat the reasons behind the hope must be given.

In general the yellow hat is looking forward into the future: 'If we do this, then these benefits will arise . . .'

The yellow hat can also be used for looking backwards into the past: 'This thing happened. There were a lot of harmful effects. But there were also some good effects – let's put on our yellow hat to find the good effects.'

The yellow-hat thinker asks himself or herself the following questions:

1. What are the benefits?

2. Why should it work?

What are the Benefits?

The yellow-hat thinker seeks to find and show the benefits. What are the benefits? For whom are the benefits? How do the benefits arise?

What are the advantages? Why is this worth doing? What is the nature of the improvement?

There may be cost savings. There may be improvements in function. There may be new opportunities opened up.

What are the values here? Who is affected by these values?

It must always be remembered that the yellow-hat thinker is looking only for the benefits or positive effects. The reason for this is that we need to provide some part of our thinking where we make this deliberate positive effort. The yellow-hat thinking is not assessing all the values but only the beneficial values.

It should be noted that if the yellow-hat thinking cannot turn up enough benefits the thing is not worth doing anyway. If such benefits can be shown, the matter still has to be assessed using the black hat.

Why Should It Work?

The yellow-hat thinker must show clearly why an idea will work. The reasons must be given. It is not up to other people to show why the idea will not work. First of all the yellow-hat thinking must examine the basis for claiming the idea will work.

Yellow-hat thinking seeks to show the feasibility of the idea and why it can be done.

Over-use:

There are people who get carried away by an idea and plunge ahead with yellow-hat thinking without facing the realities or practicalities. This is not so much over-use of the yellow hat as failure to use the black hat.

The black hat not only provides an assessment of an idea but can also point out the weaknesses of the idea so that these might be overcome.

SUMMARY

The black hat is used for judgement and assessment. The black hat is used for criticism. The black hat prevents mistakes and errors and can also lead to the improvement of ideas.

The yellow hat focuses on benefits. Can this thing be done? Is it worth doing?

Both hats are fully logical and reasons must be given.

EXERCISES ON BLACK-HAT AND YELLOW-HAT THINKING

1. Someone suggests that there should be cars specially designed for women. Do some black-hat thinking to point out the weaknesses in this idea.

2. There is a lot of stealing going on at school. Rewards are offered to anyone who can catch a thief. Is this a good idea? Do some yellow-hat thinking first and then some black-hat thinking on the idea.

3. There is a surplus of food in some countries but in other countries people are starving. Should some of the surplus food be given free to the people who are starving? Write out an imaginary conversation between one person wearing a yellow hat and another person wearing a black hat. Two points per person.

4. Which of the following are proper black-hat remarks:
'Fining people for dropping litter in the street is a police-state idea.'
'The fact that many fat people seem happy does not mean that they are fat because they are happy.'
'A publicity campaign in the newspapers won't work because many people cannot read.'
'People who tell lies are usually found out.'
'In my experience paying people higher wages does not make them happier.'
'If you do not work hard you will not get good results in the test.'

5. Use yellow-hat thinking to show the benefits in the suggestion that everyone should keep a pet of some sort.

6. If you never read newspapers and never listened to television news, what would happen? Do some yellow-hat and some black-hat thinking on this.

7. Do some yellow-hat thinking on the use of the black hat.

Green-Hat Thinking and Blue-Hat Thinking

The green hat and the blue hat are opposites in the sense that the green hat is full of energy and the freedom of thinking in any direction whereas the blue hat is concerned with the control and direction of the thinking process.

GREEN HAT

Think of grass, trees, vegetation and growth. Think of the energy of growth and fertility. Think of shoots and branches.

The green hat is the 'active' hat.

The green hat is the hat for creative thinking. In fact the green hat covers both uses of the word 'creative'.

1. Creative thinking may mean bringing something about or making something happen. This is similar to constructive thinking. The green hat is concerned with proposals and suggestions.

2. Creative thinking may mean new ideas, new alternatives, new solutions, new inventions. Here the emphasis is on 'newness'.

The white hat lays out the information. The red hat allows feelings to be put forward. The black and yellow hats deal with logical assessment. So it falls to the green hat to be the action hat under which ideas are put forward.

When you are asked to put on the green hat you are being asked to come up with suggestions and ideas. This is active thinking, not reactive thinking.

The five main uses of the green hat are as follows:

1. Exploration

2. Proposals and suggestions

3. Alternatives

4. New ideas

5. Provocations

Unlike the yellow-hat and black-hat thinkers, the green-hat thinker
does not have to come up with logical reasons to support the suggestion or idea. It is enough to put forward the idea for further examination.

Exploration:

The white hat is used to explore the situation in terms of available
information. But the green hat is used to explore the situation in
terms of ideas, concepts, suggestions and possibilities.

Proposals and Suggestions:

The green hat is used to put forward proposals or suggestions of
any sort. These do not need to be new ideas. Suggestions for action.
Proposals to solve a problem. Possible decisions. These are all part
of the active thinking that takes place under the green hat. If no one
has any ideas about what can be done then it is time for some green-
hat thinking.

Alternatives:

An explanation has been given. Or, a course of action is being
discussed. There is a green-hat request for further options or alternatives. What else can be done? What other possible explanations
might there be? The green hat seeks to broaden the range of options
before pursuing any one of them in detail. It is the role of the yellow
and black hats to assess the alternatives.

New Ideas:

Sometimes there is a need for really new ideas. The old ideas do not
work or there may be no ideas available to tackle the problem. Real
creative or lateral thinking is now needed. Such thinking is a prime
role of the green hat. If you ask someone to go away to do some
green-hat thinking on a subject, you are asking for some new ideas –
beyond the existing ones. You can never demand that someone has
new ideas but you can request that the person makes an effort. The

lateral-thinking techniques that are described later in the book can be used deliberately in order to try to generate some new ideas.

Provocations:

Under the green hat we can put forward tentative ideas. We have no idea if such ideas will work. Under the green hat we can also put forward deliberate provocations. A provocation is never meant to be a usable idea. A provocation is meant to jerk our mind out of its usual tracks so that we can see things differently. The technique of provocation is described later in the book.

Action and Energy:

Green-hat thinking is characterized by action and energy. If an artist is standing before a blank canvas the important thing is to get going. This may mean making preliminary sketches or putting something down on the canvas itself. Blank situations need ideas. Blank situations need green-hat thinking. Old situations or stagnant situations also need green-hat thinking.

BLUE HAT

Think of the blue sky. The sky is above everything. If you were up in the sky you would be looking down at everything below. With blue-hat thinking you are above the thinking: you are looking down at the thinking. With blue-hat thinking you are thinking about thinking.

The blue hat is the overview. The blue hat is the process control. The blue hat is like the conductor of the orchestra. With all the other hats we think about the subject matter, but with the blue hat we think about our thinking.

The blue hat covers the following points:

1. Where are we now?

2. What is the next step?

3. Program for thinking

4. Summary

5. Observation and comment

A person who puts on the blue hat steps back from the thinking that is going on in order to watch that thinking.

Where are We Now?

Where are we in our thinking?

What is the focus?

What are we trying to do right now?

This is an attempt to see – at this moment – what our thinking is about. Are we just drifting or trying to do something?

What is the Next Step?

What should we do next (in our thinking)?

The blue-hat thinker may suggest the use of another hat, or a summary, or a definition of the focus etc. It may be that no one knows what to do next, so a suggestion is necessary. It may be that everyone wants to do something different next, so a decision is required. If there is a clear view of the next step then that step can be taken.

Program for Thinking:

Instead of just choosing the next step, the blue hat can be used for setting out a whole program of thinking on the subject. This is an agenda or sequence in which various thinking steps will be taken. This would usually be done at the beginning of the meeting but could be done at any time. The program could cover the whole meeting or apply just to one subject or part of a subject. In some cases the program may consist of a sequence of the thinking hats.

The blue hat treats thinking in a formal manner. Just as a computer programmer sets up a program for a computer so the blue hat can set up the program for thinking.

Summary:

At any point in the thinking anyone present can put on the blue hat and ask for a summary.

. . . 'Where are we? How far have we got? Can we have a summary?'

Such a summary may give a sense of achievement but may also show how little has been achieved during the thinking. The summary may also serve to clarify the different points of view.

Observation and Comment:

The blue-hat thinker is above the thinking and looking down at what is happening. So the blue-hat thinker observes and comments.

... 'It seems to me that all we have been doing is argue about the objective of this meeting.'

... 'We set out to consider some alternatives and we have only considered one so far.'

... 'There is a lot of red-hat thinking this morning.'

This blue-hat function makes thinkers conscious of their thinking behaviour. Just how effective is it?

Over-use:

In practice many people use the blue hat without saying they are doing so. It is better to declare it openly. Over-use is not a real problem but must be avoided. It is very irritating if every few seconds someone halts the meeting to make a blue-hat comment. Occasional use is more effective.

SUMMARY

The green hat is for action and creativity: for ideas, suggestions and proposals. These do not have to be worked out in detail.

The blue hat is for the control of the thinking process itself. What has happened? What is happening? What should happen next?

EXERCISES ON GREEN-HAT AND BLUE-HAT THINKING

1. You are selling newspapers but you cannot get anyone to deliver them. Put on your green hat and make some suggestions.

2. Your dog and your neighbour's dog fight the whole time. What green-hat suggestions do you have?

3. You are running a fast-food business (pizza). A competitor opens another outlet (also pizza) near by. You start to lose business. Put on your blue hat and decide the first three steps in your thinking. How should your thinking go?

4. You do not have enough space to store your books and papers in your room. You put on your green hat and come up with the following alternatives:
... throw some of them away
... ask a friend with more space to keep them for you
What other alternatives can you think of?

5. A film-maker sets a competition to find the best idea for a monster type of film. There is a need for a new type of monster. Put on your blue hat first to see how you would set about thinking up a new monster. Then try some green-hat thinking to make suggestions for that monster.

6. There is a straight piece of road and people drive too fast along it. Pedestrians are always getting injured and even killed. Some green-hat thinking on this problem?

7. There is a search for a new shape for cereal boxes. Someone puts on a green hat and makes the provocation that cereal boxes should be round like a ball. Can you get anything useful from that provocation?

8. There is an argument between a father and daughter as to what time she should get home in the evening. Using your blue hat how would you set a program for that argument?

Six Thinking Hats in Sequence

There are two types of use for the six thinking hats:

1. Occasional use

2. Systematic (sequence) use

OCCASIONAL USE: This is the most common use. The hats are used one at a time (or two if you ask for a switch of hats). At a meeting or in a conversation someone suggests the use of one of the hats. Then the meeting or conversation continues. The hat that has been introduced is used for only two or three minutes. This occasional use of the hats allows someone to ask for a particular type of thinking or to suggest a switch in thinking. The hats provide a means for switching thinking.

SYSTEMATIC USE: Here a sequence of hats is set up in advance and the thinker goes through one hat after the other. This is sometimes done when there is a need to cover some subject quickly and effectively. In a sense the blue hat is used to set up the sequence of hats, which then becomes a program for thinking about the subject. This method is also useful if there is a quarrel or argument about a matter and no useful thinking is being done.

SEQUENCE USE

What is the correct sequence in which the six hats could be used?

There is no single correct sequence because the sequence will vary with the circumstances. You are free to make up your own sequence but some rules or guidelines are given here.

1. Each hat may be used any number of times in the sequence.

2. In general it is best to use the yellow hat before the black hat since it is difficult to be positive after you have been critical.

3. The black hat is used in two ways. The first way is to point out the weaknesses in an idea. This should then be followed by the green hat, which tries to overcome the weakness. The second use of the black hat is for assessment.

4. The black hat is always used for final assessment of the idea. This final assessment should always be followed by the red hat. This is so that we can see how we feel about the idea after we have assessed it.

5. If you believe that there are strong feelings about a subject, you would always start the thinking with the red hat in order to get those feelings out into the open.

6. If there are no strong feelings you would start with the white hat in order to collect information. After the white hat you would use the green hat to generate some alternatives. Then you would assess each alternative with the yellow hat followed by the black hat. You would then choose an alternative and finally assess your choice with the black hat followed by the red hat.

The major difference in sequence is between the two situations: seeking an idea; reacting to an idea.

Seeking an Idea:

The sequence of hat colours might be:

WHITE: To gather available information.

GREEN: For further exploration and to generate alternatives.

YELLOW: To assess the benefits and feasibility of each alternative.

BLACK: To assess the weaknesses and dangers of each alternative.

GREEN: To develop further the most promising alternatives and to make a choice.

BLUE: To summarize and assess what has been achieved so far.

BLACK: To make the final judgement on the chosen alternative.

RED: To find out the feelings on the outcome.

Reacting to a Presented Idea:

Here the sequence is different because the idea is known and, usually, the background information is also known.

RED: To find out the existing feelings about the idea.

YELLOW: To make an effort to find the benefits in the idea.

BLACK: To point out weaknesses, problems and dangers in the idea.

GREEN: To see if the idea can be modified to strengthen the yellow-hat benefits and to overcome the black-hat problems.

WHITE: To see if available information can help in modifying the idea to make it more acceptable (if the red-hat feelings are against the idea).

GREEN: Development of the final suggestion.

BLACK: Judgement of the final suggestion.

RED: To find out the feelings on the outcome.

Short Sequences:

Quite often short sequences of the hats are used for various purposes.

YELLOW/BLACK/RED: For quick assessment of an idea.

WHITE/GREEN: To generate ideas.

BLACK/GREEN: To improve an existing idea.

BLUE/GREEN: To summarize and spell out the alternatives.

BLUE/YELLOW: To see if the thinking has had any benefits.

SUMMARY

The six hats are usually used one at a time in the course of thinking. This is the occasional use.

In the systematic use a sequence of hats may be set up as a program to guide the thinking. There are guidelines about the most useful sequences.

EXERCISES ON THE SEQUENCE USE OF THE SIX HATS

1. If you could only use a sequence of three hats to find a present for your best friend's birthday, what would the sequence be?

2. There is a meeting to discuss the problem of young criminals. Which hat do you think should be used first?

3. Your family is planning to move to another part of the country. You are asked what you think about the move. What sequence of hats would you use (give the first four)?

4. A group of young people are always holding parties and the loud music is upsetting their neighbours. The neighbours have a meeting to discuss the problem. Their choice of hats is: RED/BLACK/GREEN/BLACK/RED. Do you agree with this sequence of hats? What sequence would you suggest?

5. You need to earn some money quickly in order to buy something you want very much. What sequence of hats would you set up to guide your thinking?

6. Some people do not seem to enjoy life enough. What sort of thinking should such people do? Give a short sequence of four hats.

7. For each of the following situations which hat would you use first of all:
. . . You are accused of being a liar.
. . . You break your right arm in an accident.
. . . Your mother is very ill and has to go to hospital.
. . . You find an envelope with a lot of money in it.
. . . You discover your friend is a thief.
. . . You get offered a very good summer job.

8. A man buys a car from a friend, after testing it. But after a week the car breaks down and needs expensive repairs. They meet to discuss who should pay for the repairs. Set out a sequence of hats for the discussion.

Outcome and Conclusion

... 'You have been thinking for twenty minutes – what is the outcome?'

... 'The five minutes' thinking time is up – what is the outcome?'

... 'This meeting has gone on for three hours. We have had a lot of discussion. What is the outcome?'

In general there seem to be two possible answers to that question:

... 'Here is the solution to the problem. Here is the answer. Here is the decision. Here is the conclusion.'

... 'We do not seem to have got anywhere at all.'

When the thinking has to come to an end what is the outcome? Is it just a matter of either a specific answer or nothing at all? If there is not the specific answer have we been wasting our time?

If you do not seem to be getting anywhere then thinking is not enjoyable. So it is important to pay attention to the outcome of any thinking. The outcome is not just a matter of right answer or no answer.

There are many possible outcomes of thinking, but we can simplify them into three types of outcome:

1. Better map (exploration)

2. Pin-pointing needs

3. Specific answer

BETTER MAP

At the end of your thinking you should have a better map of what you have been thinking about. If nothing else you have gone over the territory. You have explored.

You have a better idea of the information, concepts and feelings in the matter.

You should be able to list the alternatives that are available. These may be alternative views, alternative courses of action, alternative approaches, alternative values. You may not be able to decide upon them or come to a conclusion, but at least you are now aware of these alternatives. That is worth something.

Sometimes the specific purpose of the thinking is to explore a subject. So exploration does have a certain value.

The key question to ask yourself (as a habit) is:

'What have I found out? What do I know now that I did not know when I started?'

PIN-POINTING NEEDS

After thinking about a matter you should have a much clearer idea about why you cannot go further, about why you cannot reach a conclusion.

It may be that there is a need for some vital information and you cannot proceed without that.

. . . 'Without that information we cannot proceed.'

It may be that you have narrowed down the problem to a specific difficulty – you have pin-pointed the sticking point.

. . . 'The sticking point is that we have no way of telling which of these new chemicals will work in the actual situation.'

Pin-pointing a need or a sticking point is a considerable achievement. You have not yet got the final answer but you have moved a step closer. You now know better what you have to do next. You have to find the needed information. You have to overcome the sticking point. Your thinking can now be much more focused.

The key question to ask yourself (as a habit) is:

'What is the sticking point? What is holding us up?'

SPECIFIC ANSWER

This means that you have come to a conclusion; have reached a decision; have arrived at a design; have a specific plan or strategy; have a solution to the problem; have an answer to the question.

In a mathematics problem at school when you get an answer you can often check if it is the right answer. Most of life is not like that. When you get an answer it may seem very likely to you that the answer will work. Or it may merely seem probable that the answer might work. Or you think there is some chance the answer might work. Or it is the best answer you can find and you do not really know if it is going to work.

There is some merit in coming to a definite conclusion even if it is only the best you can do.

The key questions to ask yourself (as a habit) are:

'What is my answer (or conclusion)?'

'Why do I think it will work?'

SUMMARY

At the end of any thinking session you need to make an effort to define the outcome of your thinking.

If you have no specific answer you ask:

'What have I found out?'

'What is the sticking point?'

If you do have a specific answer you ask:

'What is my answer?'

'Why do I think my answer will work?'

These questions should become part of the general habits of thinking. This means the questions should be applied routinely at the end of all thinking.

THE FIVE-MINUTE THINKING FORMAT

This format can be used for practising thinking in order to develop thinking skills. It can be used for practising thinking at odd times. The format can also be used for serious thinking about a subject.

The time discipline is very important, since this is what forces the thinking to concentrate on thinking. The time should be strictly set by a watch and the different stages indicated. It is much less valuable if you just set out to think for 'roughly five minutes'. In using the format for the purposes of this book I strongly suggest that accurate timing is kept.

One Minute

Be clear about the purpose of the thinking.

Be clear about the focus.

Be clear about the sort of outcome you need.

Be clear about the situation.

If not enough information has been given you, do not waste time asking questions. Instead, set your own circumstances and then give these when you give the answer. For example, if the problem is about a boy who steals, you may want to know the age of the boy and how often he has stolen. So you say: 'I am assuming this boy is fourteen and this is the first time he has stolen.'

Next Two Minutes

First of all you explore the subject in terms of information and your own experience. Then you start to have some ideas.

Finally you try to condense your ideas into a number of alternatives. These alternatives may be courses of action or solutions to a problem.

Later in this book there will be some tools that will help with this stage of thinking. For the moment it is enough to use your existing thinking skills.

At the end of the two minutes you should have some alternatives.

The sort of questions that might help you are:

Is there an obvious answer?

What are the usual answers here?

In very broad terms what would I like to do?

How can I put that wish into practical action?

What other ways are there?

Next One Minute

This is the stage of choosing or deciding. At the end of the previous stage you should have put forward some alternatives. Now you have to decide between them. The sort of questions that might help you are:

Which alternative is most likely to work?

Which alternative would be most acceptable in practice?

Which alternative best fits my needs and priorities?

Which alternative best fits the circumstances of this thinking exercise?

The particular circumstances of the thinking exercise are important. You may be expected to come up with the most sound answer – even if this is well known. At other times you may be expected to come up with an original idea – even if this may not work.

Final One Minute

If you have reached a conclusion, answer or decision, test it out by going through the reasons why you think it will work. You may have time to compare it with other possible solutions to show why the one you chose is better.

If you do not have a final conclusion, you should spend this minute defining the outcome of your thinking in another way.

What have you learned through thinking about the subject?

What alternatives have you considered (even if you could not decide between them)?

What alternative approaches might there be – even if these are not solutions?

What further information do you really need?

What are the sticking points?

What are the key problems?

Output

At the end of the five minutes you must be able to give your output. You must be able to do this directly without waiting to be asked questions.

EXERCISES ON THE FIVE-MINUTE THINKING FORMAT

1. Do a five-minute format on the following situation. Your neighbour's guests always park their cars in front of the garage of your house so that the garage cannot be used. What can be done about it?

2. Do a five-minute format on the following situation. A survey shows that most people eat far too much and are overweight. What can be done about that?

3. Do a five-minute format on the following situation. A girl feels that a teacher is being very unfair to her – what can she do?

4. A factory produces a rather bad smell. The company that owns the factory is getting lots of complaints from the people living around. When the factory was built there were no houses near by. Now there are many. What should the owners of the factory do? Try a five-minute format and give your outcome.

5. If man had been in charge of the path of evolution and had been able to choose whether to live on land or in the water like dolphins – what might have happened? Try a five-minute format and give an outcome.

6. Do a five-minute format on how you would treat young criminals (aged fourteen to seventeen).

7. A friend of yours wants to hold a party at her home but her mother has forbidden it. Do a five-minute format on how you might solve this problem.

Forward or Parallel

There are two main directions of thinking: forward or parallel.

You can walk along the path, or you can pause and look around at the garden.

The diagram on p. 108 illustrates the difference between forward and parallel. In forward thinking if we are at A we move forward to B and then to C. If we have both A and B then we move forward to C. In other words where we get to is determined by where we are now.

In parallel thinking we have A and then B and then C, all in parallel. They are not determined by each other. They exist in parallel. We can look around to find them.

There is food on the table. And we are hungry. So let us sit down to eat. This is forward thinking.

In parallel thinking we might say: there is bread on the table; there is butter on the table; there is soup on the table etc., etc. All these exist in parallel.

Strangers standing around in a crowd are parallel. A woman moving towards someone she recognizes as a friend is 'forward'.

The key question for parallel thinking is:

What else is there?

This means what other things, what other alternatives, what other points of view, what other perceptions etc., etc.

The key question for forward thinking is:

So what follows?

If we have 'this' then what follows? Where do we go from here? What can we deduce?

A person enters a room and looks around. He notices law books on

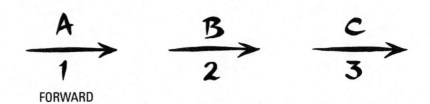

FORWARD

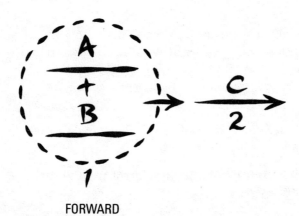

FORWARD

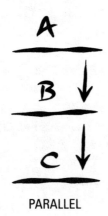

PARALLEL

the shelves so he concludes that the user of the room is a lawyer. This is forward thinking.

Another person enters the same room and looks around. She notices the pictures on the wall, the colour of the carpet, the law books, the elegant desk, the family photograph, and the cat in the corner. This is parallel thinking. If this person had wanted to deduce the occupation of the person using the room, she would also have suggested a lawyer. But that was not the type of thinking she was using.

Both forward and parallel thinking are important. Neither one is better than the other. The important thing is to recognize and use both types.

Sometimes parallel thinking has been called 'divergent' thinking, but I feel that term can give the wrong impression of moving away from something. Similarly, forward thinking is sometimes called 'convergent' thinking. Forward and parallel seem simpler terms: we move forward or we look around.

It is obvious that $5 + 3$ give the answer 8. That is forward thinking.

The answer 8 could have been the result of $5 + 3$. But it could also have been the result of $4 + 4$, $7 + 1$ and $6 + 2$. This is parallel thinking.

We use parallel thinking for exploring both what is there and also possibilities.

We use forward thinking for going forward to solutions or conclusions.

The two key questions to ask as a habit of thinking are:

What else might there be?

So what follows?

LOGIC AND PERCEPTION

The traditional emphasis in thinking has always been on logic. This is not surprising. Thinking in education is almost always reactive. How do you respond to what is placed before you? So the information is given. The pieces of the puzzle are given. You use logic to work out the answer.

Critical thinking, argument and the adversarial system are largely (not entirely) based on logic.

Logic is the way scientists, or other people, have to present their ideas. Even if a scientific breakthrough came out through hunch or chance it must be presented as if it were the result of logic. Otherwise ideas cannot be accepted.

We need to see how conclusions have been reached, so we need to see the reasons or logic behind them.

For all these reasons we have come to put a lot of emphasis on logic.

You wake up at night in a strange hotel room. You want to go to the bathroom but you cannot find the light switch. You reckon that if you feel your way around the wall you must find a door that leads to the bathroom – or if you find any other door there will probably be a light switch near to it. This is normal logical thinking.

But if you had found the light switch by the bed, you would have been able to find your way to the bathroom without any extra logic. Being able to see your way to the bathroom corresponds to perception.

Sometimes we need logic to take our perceptions further. Sometimes better perception reduces the need for logic.

Perception is how we see the world around us.

Logic is how we make the best use of those perceptions.

Most often the perceptions are converted into the form of language or symbols. We then use the rules of logic in language or mathematics to move forward to some conclusion.

I once observed a cicada at close range. The cicada was making a loud noise but I could not tell how the noise was being made. No matter how closely I looked at the cicada I could not see any wings, wing cases or legs moving in such a way as to make the noise. It was only later that I found that another cicada, a few inches away on the other side of the branch, was actually making the noise. This example is typical of one of the most widespread errors in thinking. If we look at only part of the situation, our logic will give us a false answer. But how do we know that there is more that we should be looking at? That is where perception comes in.

Wisdom is directly based on perception. Wisdom is the ability to take in many things. Things that are now present and things that will happen in the future. Wisdom allows us to look at things in different ways.

The two main aspects of perception are: breadth and change.

So the key habit questions to ask are:

How broad a view am I taking?

In what other ways is it possible to look at things?

Change is the ability to look at exactly the same thing but in a different way.

One shoe salesman wrote: 'This is a terrible market – no one wears shoes.' The other salesman wrote: 'This is a wonderful market – no one wears shoes.'

CAF: Consider All Factors

This is one of the thinking tools from the widely used CoRT Thinking Program (published by SRA) that I developed. This program is now in use in thousands of schools world-wide. The CoRT Program is a comprehensive program consisting of sixty thinking lessons divided into six sections. There are detailed teacher guides.

A small handful of the CoRT tools are included in this book because it would be confusing to create new tools to serve the same purpose. I must make clear, however, that the full CoRT Program is the one designed for educational use in schools. This book is designed for parents at home. It may also happen that parents who use this book may want to move on to the full CoRT Program.

CAF is an attention-directing tool. CAF is a tool designed to increase the breadth of perception. What are the factors that have to be considered in this matter?

CAF is pronounced 'caff'.

... 'Please do a "caff" on this.'

... 'If you had done a "caff" you would not have left out that important point.'

... 'Should we do a CAF here?'

The more you use the tool in a deliberate manner the more of a tool it becomes. If you are shy about mentioning the tool, it does not become usable as a tool but remains as a weak attitude.

A father told his young daughter that she could call in early at his office on her way back from school, because business was very slack. When she arrived at his office the girl (who had been doing CoRT Thinking at school) suggested to her father that they do a CAF on why business was slack. Some ideas were developed that helped the business to pick up again.

Looking around a used-car lot a man suddenly spots his favourite make of sports car. The condition is good, the mileage is right and the price is just affordable. He is delighted. Later he comes back and purchases the car. He drives home in triumph. He then finds that the car is too wide to fit in the garage at his home. He had forgotten to do a CAF.

A dwarf got into the elevator intending to go up to the twentieth floor. But he had to get out at the tenth floor. He could only reach as high as the tenth-floor button. He had not done a CAF. If he had, he might have waited until someone else was ready to get into the elevator.

The government allowed wealthy foreigners to bid up the price of houses in the town. They then found that they could not get local people to work in the town – because the local people could not afford the same prices. Someone had not done a CAF.

Teaching CAF is a matter of adding to the list of factors.

What has been left out?

Can you add another factor to the list we have?

What else must be considered?

Of course, there is a difference between important factors and less important factors. But the main effort is to find the factors. Far too often we go ahead with our thinking without having done a proper CAF.

Although CAF is a very simple tool it can be very powerful when it is done well.

EXERCISES ON CAF

1. A lion-tamer in a circus has lost one of his lions in an accident. He has to replace this lion. Do a CAF for him. What factors must he take into account?

2. You are asked to design an advertisement to get young people to drink more Coke. What factors do you have to keep in mind? Do a CAF.

3. A herd of wild horses roams freely over some grazing lands. Dead

horses are found and the farmers are accused of shooting the horses. The farmers claim that there are now too many horses and they are taking the grazing from the cattle. Do a CAF on this situation.

4. You are going to a job interview. What things do you have to keep in mind? Do a CAF.

5. Your parents are choosing a place to go on holiday. They have done a CAF and list the following factors. Have they left out anything?
cost
climate
good restaurants
nearness to a beach
sporting facilities

6. A friend asks to borrow some money from you. You do a CAF and list the following factors. Are these enough?
the amount of money
how long he wants the money for
how good a friend he is

7. If you had to make suggestions for re-designing the human head and face, what factors would you keep in mind? Do a CAF on this.

8. You are running a large department store and you want to recruit some new staff. When interviewing the applicants what factors would you consider?

APC: Alternatives, Possibilities, Choices

This is another attention-directing tool. Instead of moving 'forward' with our thinking we look at 'parallel' possibilities.

A lot of humour is based on alternatives. The simple pun is based on alternative meanings of the same word. A rich man complained that he had had a miserable birthday because he was only given a golf club – and it did not even have a swimming pool.

A famous advertising slogan read: 'Nothing works faster than Anacin'. This is meant to mean that no treatment acts faster (to cure a headache) than does Anacin. It could also mean that 'nothing' (taking nothing) has a quicker effect on headaches than taking Anacin.

There are many sorts of alternatives:

PERCEPTION: The same thing can be looked at in many different ways.

ACTION: Alternative courses of action that can be taken in a situation.

SOLUTIONS: Alternative solutions to a problem.

APPROACHES: Different ways of tackling the problem in order to find a solution.

EXPLANATIONS: Alternative explanations of how something happened. Alternative hypotheses in science.

DESIGN: Alternative designs, each of which fulfils the purpose of the design (machines, buildings, posters etc.).

Sometimes we are forced to look for alternatives because the traditional way does not work. Sometimes we want to look for alternatives because we believe we might find a better way than the one we now use.

If someone tells you that there are only two possible solutions to a problem, you might spend a few moments thinking of further altern-atives. You may or may not find further alternatives, but it is always worth spending some time looking for them.

Perhaps the most difficult thing to do is to stop to look for altern-atives when you do not have to. Gillette invented the safety razor when he stopped to look for an alternative way of shaving. We often assume that things are done in the best possible way, but that is not always so. Often things are done in that way for historical reasons or because no one has tried to find a better way.

Whenever you set out to look for alternatives you must be very clear about the purpose of the alternative.

. . . 'I want alternative ways of blocking this hole.'

. . . 'I want alternative ways of carrying water to that point.'

. . . 'I want alternative suggestions as to how this system might fail.'

'I want alternative colours for the carpet' is quite different from 'I want alternative ways of covering the floor'. If you just say, 'I want alternatives to a carpet,' it is not clear whether you want alternative ways of covering the floor or alternatives that are as warm as a carpet.

The APC is pronounced with each letter separate: 'A', 'P', 'C', or A.P.C. As with CAF, the more formally and the more deliberately the tool is used the more valuable it becomes as a tool.

EXERCISES ON APC

1. If some mysterious disease suddenly made the majority of people deaf, how would people communicate with each other? Do an APC and give more than three alternatives.

2. In some countries motorists pay tolls for using the roads. What other ways are there for getting motorists to pay for the roads they use? Do an APC.

3. You receive a mysterious telephone call asking you to meet someone you do not know at a certain time in a coffee shop. What are the possible explanations for this? What courses of action do you have? Do a double APC.

4. In a TV quiz show an object is described as being: round, flat and good to eat. It could be a hamburger, or what else? Do an APC listing as many possibilities as you can think of.

5. A man is seen walking down the high street with a brown paper bag over his head. Why do you think he is doing this? Do an APC and list at least five possible explanations.

6. You form a group with your friends to raise money for charity. You have just one day to raise as much money as you can. Do an APC and give some alternative approaches to this task.

7. Some neighbourhoods are very dirty because people drop litter and cans everywhere. How would you suggest tackling this problem? Do an APC and give three approaches.

8. You are running an insurance company and your salespeople have worked very hard. You want to reward them. You could give them more money as a bonus but you want to find other ways of rewarding them. Do an APC and suggest some alternative rewards.

9. Can you think of an alternative shape for a TV screen? If you can, use yellow-hat thinking to show the benefits of your new shape.

Values

In mathematics and in logic puzzles it is enough to get the right answer. Real life is very different because values are involved. Values are part of thinking. Values usually involve other people. A logically correct solution to a problem may be unacceptable because it goes against people's values (which may be illogical).

If we are going to think in the real world, we have to be conscious of values in all our thinking.

A wide new highway is built leading into the city. Let us look at the people and values involved.

... the farmers whose land is taken over by the new road are not happy.
... neighbours who are now separated by the new road are not happy.
... those who find themselves alongside the new road are upset by the noise and the pollution and danger to their children.
... those who live outside the city are delighted to be able to drive in more quickly.
... some people now living in the city are delighted to move out to the country where houses are cheaper and the quality of life is better.
... city people can drive out to the country more often.
... there is more traffic congestion in the city because more people now drive in every day.
... there is more pollution from car exhausts.
... there is more energy consumption and the need to import more oil.
... dealers can sell bigger and faster cars.
... some people in the country can now sell their houses at a higher price than before.
... village schools are saved because there are now more pupils.

Not all situations are as complex as this but all situations do involve different values for different people. The world is quite a crowded place. What is good for one person may be bad for another. A new airport is good for those who have to fly but bad for those who live nearby and suffer from the noise.

Drugs and cosmetics are tested on animals to be sure they are safe for human use. That is good for humans but bad for animals.

If you give free food to starving countries, that is good for the people but bad for the local farmers who cannot sell their produce. In the long run this may be bad for all the people as farming declines.

In all thinking there are two key questions which should become a thinking habit. These questions should be asked routinely whenever we are thinking about something:

1. What are the values involved?

2. Who is affected by the values?

Both yellow-hat and black-hat thinking are concerned with values. With yellow-hat thinking we look for the benefits. With black-hat thinking we look for the problems and dangers.

In looking at values we need to look at the people involved. The specific OPV tool is explained in the next few pages.

In looking at values we need to look at the consequences of any action. The specific C&S tool is explained in the next few pages.

In looking at values we need a quick way of assessing the plus, minus and interesting aspects. The specific PMI tool is explained in the next few pages.

EXERCISES ON VALUES

1. You enjoy watching television. Your parents think you watch far too much. What are the values involved?

2. A lawyer knows that her client is guilty of a robbery. Should she defend him in court? What are the values involved?

3. In cartoons and in real life, dogs do not like cats and mice do not like cats. But some people like cats. What are all the values involved here?

4. In some countries women work at home for a very low wage

sewing clothes. What do you think about the following values?
... at least the women have some income
... the children get some food to eat
... the wages are too low and the women are exploited
... the employer wants to make a profit from the selling of the clothes
... the shops in your country want to sell the clothes
... you like the cheap clothes and want to buy them

5. There is a rise in street crime (muggings etc.). Who are the people involved or affected by this? What are the values?

6. People enjoy gossiping about each other even if the things that are said are not always true. Who is involved in gossip and what are the values?

7. Someone you know is bored at school and spends all the time working in a café to earn money. Who are the people involved and what are the values?

8. In Japan there are less than 2,000 murders a year. In the USA the population is double that of Japan and there are about 28,000 murders a year. What values are involved?

9. Your father does not like your new friend. You have a fight with your father. What are the values involved?

OPV: Other People's Views

This is another attention-directing tool designed to broaden perception. It is pronounced: 'O', 'P', 'V', or O.P.V.

... 'There are lots of people involved, let's do an OPV.'

... 'You would not be in this mess if you had done an OPV.'

Imagine a boxing match for the world heavyweight championship. One of the fighters throws an uppercut. His opponent is knocked out. There is a new world champion.

In thinking that is to be followed by action there is usually someone who does something and someone else (or many others) who is affected by the action – as in the boxing match. In that match, however, there were many other people affected, not just the fighters. There were the spectators, there were the media (TV and newspapers), there were those who made bets, there was the next challenger, the promoters etc., etc. In the same way action can affect many other people apart from those directly concerned. So thinking about the action must also consider these other people. So the OPV is an important thinking tool.

The world is full of people. Thinking is done by people. Thinking affects people.

The two key questions are:

1. Who is affected by this thinking (action)?

2. What are the views (thinking) of those affected?

The OPV and values are very closely linked because the views of those affected are going to be determined by the values involved. So in doing an OPV we need to look closely at the values involved.

Can people look after their own values? They may not have the knowledge. The long-term consequences of building a dam in a certain place may be very complex. People may over-react out of ignorance or under-react. Future generations should also come into the OPV. They cannot be present to do their own thinking, so part of the OPV is on their behalf.

There is also long-term thinking and short-term thinking. A rise in food prices may be very unpopular in the short term. But long term this rise may benefit farmers who are motivated to produce more food, so eventually all benefit.

Keep in mind that the OPV is always concerned with what other people actually think at this moment – not with what they should think. Also an OPV is about the specific views of other people. You must put yourself in the shoes of these other people to think and feel as they do. The OPV is not just a matter of alternative views on the subject. It is views held by specific people.

The first step in doing an OPV is always to list the people affected. The second step is to imagine the views and thinking of each of these people (or groups). In some cases the list of people could extend almost for ever. As usual you have to be reasonable about this – there is no need always to consider even those who are only slightly affected.

TWO SIDES IN AN ARGUMENT

One obvious use of the OPV is to consider the thinking of both sides in an argument or conflict. If you are on one side of the conflict, you make an effort to see things from the other side.

This effort to see the other point of view or other perception of the situation must be objective. How do they see things?

EXERCISES ON OPV

1. A beautiful tree in the garden next door grows bigger and bigger and finally cuts out the sunlight from the living room of your house. Do an OPV on the people involved. One day there is a great storm and the tree blows down, damaging your house. Do another OPV.

2. A girl gives some money to her friend to buy a lottery ticket. The friend buys two tickets. One of the tickets wins a great deal of

money. Which girl does the winning ticket belong to? Do an OPV on this.

3. A boy likes to study listening to loud music. He does not want to use earphones. His parents and his sister like to work in peace and quiet. Do an OPV.

4. A ban is suggested on all cars and trucks at all times in the centre of the city. List all the people who are going to be affected by this ban (first part of an OPV).

5. While you are ill in bed your best friend goes off with your boy-friend (or girl-friend as appropriate). Do an OPV.

6. Your grandmother aged seventy-five wants to come and live with the family. Do an OPV for your father, mother, and other members of your family (the grandmother is your mother's mother).

7. A girl who wants to get her own way goes on a hunger strike and refuses to eat anything. Do an OPV.

8. There is an increase in local taxes to pay for better education. List all the people involved and do an OPV on their views.

9. The workers in a factory want an increase in wages because the cost of living has gone up. The management say they cannot increase wages because foreign competitors are lowering the price of the same products. Do an OPV on these opposing views.

C&S: Consequence and Sequel

Never mind about the 'sequel' part, treat this perception tool as 'consequences'. The tool is pronounced 'C and S'.

You could make a case for saying that this is the most important of all the thinking tools in real life. If your thinking is going to result in action of any sort (decisions, choices, plans, initiatives etc.) then that action is going to take place in the future. So you have to look at the consequences of that action.

Will it work out?

What are the benefits?

What are the problems and dangers (risks)?

What are the costs?

The C&S is both exploration (into the future) and also evaluation. It is something like making a road map. If you see that the road ahead is a bad one, you do not take that road.

Even if the C&S were used by itself and used effectively, this alone would have a powerful effect on thinking skills.

Young people often have a great deal of trouble with the C&S. This is because they do not usually think of the future. The future is vague and far away. Next week is the maximum length of future. Also, someone else is looking after them and doing future thinking for them.

There is a relationship between C&S, CAF and OPV. What happens in the future may be considered as a factor. What happens in the future will affect other people. What happens in the future is also a matter of values. The black hat and the yellow hat can also be used to assess future consequences.

In doing a C&S you should also keep in mind 'position'. Something you do may put you in a better 'position' to do something else. For example you go to work for a TV station at very poor wages. But you are now on the spot and in a better position to become a TV journalist.

TIME SCALE

IMMEDIATE: The immediate consequences of the action.

SHORT-TERM: What happens after the immediate.

MEDIUM-TERM: What happens when things have settled down.

LONG-TERM: What happens much later.

The actual timings will vary from situation to situation. For example with a new electric power station, immediate is five years, short-term is ten years, medium-term is twenty years and long-term is up to fifty years. With a quarrel with your friend, immediate is now, short-term is one day, medium-term is one week, and long-term is one month.

For each situation set the specific time scales before starting to do the C&S.

RISK

Will it work out as I hope it will?

What might go wrong?

What are the actual dangers?

Another way of looking at risk is to ask yourself:

What is the worst thing that can go wrong?

If you can imagine the worst and still face it, you may want to go ahead with your action.

You could also ask:

What is the ideal (best) outcome?

In between these two you might ask:

What is the most likely outcome?

CERTAINTY

You can never be certain about the future. You can never have full information about the future. That is one of the reasons why thinking is so important. When we look at the future with a C&S there are different levels of certainty or uncertainty.

I am sure that things will turn out like this.

This is the most likely outcome.

It could be like this, or like this.

This is a possibility – but I cannot be sure.

I have no idea what will happen.

We often do have to act with low levels of certainty. We cannot always wait for full certainty (which may never become available). The important point is to be aware of the level of certainty. If you really are guessing – then know that you are guessing.

EXERCISES ON C&S

1. What would happen if there was a method for teaching dogs to speak? Do a C&S on this: look at immediate and long-term consequences.

2. With increasing automation it is possible that in the future people will need to work only three hours a day. What do you think would happen? Do a long-term C&S on this.

3. Supposing some research shows that watching TV for hours on end is bad for the brain. Do a C&S (immediate and short-term) on this.

4. A new law is passed that children over the age of ten are required to work ten hours a week. Do a full C&S on this.

5. Your best friend with whom you do everything is involved in a serious car accident. Your friend goes into hospital and is going to be there for six months. Do a full C&S on how this will affect your life.

6. New evidence shows that the greenhouse effect (warming up of

the earth's atmosphere) is going to occur much earlier than expected. What effect to you think this news will have on the thinking of politicians? Do a C&S with respect to politicians.

7. A new medicine is discovered that will allow people to live to the age of one hundred years. This medicine is extremely expensive. Do a full C&S.

8. There is another OPEC type crisis and the price of gasoline is suddenly trebled. Do an immediate and short-term C&S.

9. There is a mysterious and very severe illness that is caused by kissing. There is an outbreak in the town where you live. Do an immediate and short-term C&S.

PMI: Plus, Minus and Interesting

Many highly intelligent people use their thinking to back up or defend their immediate judgement of a matter. The PMI is a perception-broadening tool (attention-directing) which forces a thinker to explore the situation before coming to a judgement.

An explorer returns from an expedition with a very incomplete description of a new island. The explorer is told to go back and to describe what is to be found in the north, the east, the south, the west and the centre of the island. The explorer follows this simple attention-directing framework.

The PMI is a similar attention-directing framework. Look at the plus points. Look at the minus points. Look at the interesting points. Only when this full scan has been carried out, reach a judgement or decision.

In practice the PMI is very popular with youngsters because it is so simple and so effective. Even if the PMI alone is used without any further tools, thinking becomes much more effective in real-life situations. Youngsters often get their parents to do a PMI on matters requiring decisions or on instant reactions.

. . . 'I know you don't like this, but let's do a PMI.'

. . . 'That seems the right choice, but let's do a PMI.'

. . . 'We have two options. Let's do a PMI on each.'

The PMI is pronounced 'P', 'M', 'I', or P.M.I.

The PMI is an exploring tool and also an evaluation tool. Let us see what we will see if we look in all directions.

At first sight the PMI may look like a mini-version of the six thinking hats. It resembles the yellow hat, black hat and green hat (interesting). There is a resemblance, but the PMI is directly concerned with good (plus), bad (minus) and interesting points. The black hat is not concerned with minus points directly but with judgement of how something fits facts or experience. Also the black and yellow hats do have to be logical, whereas the PMI does not – and can even include feelings.

The PMI is a very simple, overall, exploration scan.

INTERESTING

... 'Interesting to see what would happen ...'

... 'Interesting to see what this might lead to ...'

... 'What would happen if ...'

You can use phrases like this in order to collect the interesting points. Interesting points are neither good nor bad but points of interest. Interesting points are observations and comments. Neutral points (neither good nor bad) also come under interesting.

SCAN

The PMI is a scanning tool. It is not a matter of thinking of the points as they come up and then dropping each point into a box labelled, P, M or I. It is a matter of specifically looking in the Plus direction first and noting what you see (ignore any other points); then looking specifically in the Minus direction and noting what you see (ignore any other points); and finally looking specifically in the Interesting direction.

Always keep the PMI sequence in that order (Plus points first, then Minus, then Interesting).

EXERCISES ON PMI

1. In many countries there is an increasing number of old people. There is a suggestion that there should be a specific political party representing people over sixty years old. Do a PMI on this suggestion.

2. A few companies have started a system in which each executive

at the beginning of the day can press a button to light a green or red light against his name on a board. The red light means that he is busy and stressed and does not want to be bothered. The green light means he is full of energy and ready for anything. Do a PMI on this idea. Do another PMI on this idea applied to a family – each member of the family would have a choice of the two lights every day.

3. Some cities have tried free white bicycles which belong to everyone. You pick up a bicycle and use it and then leave it for someone else to use. Do a PMI on this idea.

4. Suppose that telepathy worked and that you could tell exactly what other people were thinking when they were thinking about you. Do a PMI on this. Is it a good idea?

5. Should students vote on their teachers every year at school and give the teachers a rating? Do a PMI on this idea.

6. Some factories are trying a four-day working week in which people work for ten hours a day on four days and then have three days off. Do a PMI on this. Decide whether you think it is a good idea.

7. A mother thinks that her children are watching too much TV so she puts a coin box on the TV set and anyone who wants to watch must pay per hour. Do a PMI on this idea.

8. What do you think of the idea that for one full week each year the children should run the house completely – including shopping, cooking, cleaning etc.? Do a PMI.

Focus and Purpose

Most thinking just wanders along from point to point. The thinker lets each point suggest the next point. In a conversation what someone says triggers what other people think and say. There is a sort of vague and general notion of the subject matter and the purpose of the thinking – but this is very much in the background. This is one of the major causes of inefficiency and ineffectiveness in thinking.

Having looked at some thinking tools and some thinking habits it is now time to consider 'focus and purpose'. This is another thinking habit. This means that we should routinely be conscious of focus and purpose in all our thinking. A habit is something that should be part of all our thinking. A tool is something we choose to use on occasions. There are some related tools (AGO and FIP) and these will be considered in the next few pages.

In a furniture showroom I am considering buying a new dining-room table. I am focusing on the table. But right now I am looking at the table legs – are they sturdy enough? Then I look at the surface of the table – is it likely to stain or be damaged by hot things? My attention is caught by a scratch mark on the surface. The point is that my over-all objective is to consider buying the table. But at any point my thinking may be focused on a smaller point within that over-all objective. Not only is my thinking focused on a smaller point but the thinking about that smaller point has its own defined purpose (is this scratch significant?).

It is not enough to have a general sense of the objective of the thinking. We need to know at each moment what the focus is and what we are trying to do. This requires a certain amount of discipline and a certain amount of blue-hat thinking. We need to stand back from our thinking in order to see what is happening.

KEY QUESTIONS

All thinking habits have some key questions that we should be asking ourselves all the time. For focus and purpose these are:

What am I looking at (thinking about) right now?

What am I trying to do?

You can ask yourself such questions from time to time in your thinking. You can raise such questions at a meeting which seems to be getting nowhere.

SETTING THE FOCUS

Just as we need to be aware of the focus and purpose so we should also be able to set the focus and purpose.

What do you want to focus on?

Both from moment to moment and also in setting a thinking agenda (blue hat) you should be able to pick out and define different focus areas – and what you want to do with each focus area.

TYPE OF THINKING

We can consider four broad types of thinking:

EXPLORING: Looking around, increasing our knowledge and aware-ness of the subject. We want to make a better map of it.

SEEKING: Here we have a definite need. We want something. We want to end up with something specific. We may need a solution for a problem. We may need a design or a new creative idea. We may need to resolve a conflict. This is very different from just exploring. In this context the word 'seeking' also means 'constructing'. It is not as if the solution lies hidden somewhere and we just have to find it. We have to construct the solution just as we have to put together a design. So we talk of 'seeking to come up with the desired outcome'.

CHOOSING: There are a number of alternatives and we have to make a choice or decision. There might be just one action course and our choice is whether to use it or not. To some extent choosing comes into most thinking. For example in design or in problem-solving we reach the point where there are several possible alternatives and we have to choose between them.

ORGANIZING: Here all the pieces are present just as the pieces of a puzzle might all be present. We have to put the pieces together in the most effective way. We move things around. We try one way or another. We use various thinking tools (APC, OPV, C&S etc.). Designing a house is part of creative thinking and part of 'seeking' thinking. Putting the house up is part of organizing thinking. Laying out a plan and carrying out the plan can both be part of organizing thinking.

CHECKING: Is this correct? Is this right? Does it fit the evidence? Is it safe? Is it acceptable? This is black-hat thinking or critical thinking. We react to what is put before us. We judge it. We check it. Obviously there is a certain amount of checking that goes into all thinking (problem solutions, designs, choices, organizing etc.), but this type of thinking also exists in its own right.

It can be useful as part of focus/purpose to be aware of the type of thinking that is being done.

EXERCISES ON FOCUS AND PURPOSE

1. A designer is designing a new cup. What five aspects of a cup might she focus on? For example she might focus on the handle.

2. In a discussion on growing grapes in California the thinking seems to be focusing on the width of the space running between the vines. What do you think might be the purpose of this focus?

3. You are going to prepare a meal for three of your friends. List five things you might focus on. For example you might focus on where you are going to eat the meal.

4. You bought a cassette player from a store. The quality is not what you had expected. You want to take the player back. What should you focus on?

5. You are having a party at home for twenty of your friends. But another twenty uninvited guests turn up. These are people you

know but are not friends of yours. What should you focus on and what is the purpose of your thinking for each focus?

6. An entrepreneur is setting up an ice-cream shop in your area. He focuses upon the following points:
quality of product
known brand image
advertising and publicity
getting good staff
What else should he focus on?

7. A friend of yours has lost a pet dog of which she is very fond. You go over to help her. What are the three most important things to focus on?

8. A bad highway accident in which a coach is involved means that a lot of seriously injured people are taken to the nearest hospital. What should the chief of the hospital focus on?

AGO: Aims, Goals and Objectives

Pronounce this tool: 'A', 'G', 'O', or A.G.O.

This is another of the CoRT perception-broadening, attention-directing tools.

AGO is related to the thinking habit of wanting to know the focus and purpose of thinking at every moment. AGO, however, is more concerned with the over-all purpose or objective of the thinking than the moment-to-moment focus.

... 'You have called this meeting. I want to know what is the exact objective of our thinking here. I am asking you to do an AGO.'

... 'We have been talking for an hour but I still don't know what we are trying to achieve. Can we, please, do an AGO?'

... 'It is quite clear that your AGO is very different from mine. Perhaps we ought to sort that out before going any further.'

... 'When he took that money I think he just acted impulsively. I am sure he would not have taken it if he had done an AGO.'

Do not try to make a distinction between 'aims', 'goals' and 'objectives'. Such a distinction can be made but it is not helpful and is likely to be confusing.

What is the objective of our thinking?

What do we want to end up with?

As soon as you have a clear view of the ideal outcome of your thinking effort – then you have a clear AGO.

... 'I want to end up with a solution to the problem of young people taking drugs.'

... 'I want to end up with a way of keeping drug pushers away from school.'

... 'I want to end up with a way of convincing young people that drugs are dangerous.'

All the above are clearly specified objectives. They are all within the same area. A broad problem may be broken down into separate problems each of which is tackled as a distinct problem.

ALTERNATIVE DEFINITIONS OF THE OBJECTIVE

An AGO is often a matter for discussion. Someone may do an AGO and others may not be happy with the definition of the objective that has been suggested. It is always worth trying alternative definitions. There is no one right way of defining a problem (until after you have solved it) but some ways are much more helpful than others.

SUB-OBJECTIVES

On the way to a distant town there may be other towns that we pass through on the way. So we may set up sub-objectives on the way to solving the over-all problem. This is related both to breaking down the big problem into smaller ones and also to picking out focus areas. Deciding between these definitions is not important. What is important is to know the objective of the thinking that is taking place.

What is the objective of our thinking?

What is the focus at this moment?

EXERCISES ON AGO

1. Three cars have run into each other at a busy intersection. No one is badly hurt. What is your AGO if you are a police officer who arrives at the scene?

2. Too many aeroplanes are flying in the skies. The airports and air traffic control are congested. There are long delays and the danger of collisions. You are invited to join a team set up to think about this problem. What should the AGO of the team

be? Also break down the over-all problem into three smaller problems.

3. You think that the clothes your friend is wearing do not suit her at all. Do an AGO on this.

4. One of your group is telling lies about you. You do not know who it is. What is your real AGO here?

5. Why do young people go to school? Do an AGO for parents. Do an AGO for teachers. Do an AGO for society in general. Do an AGO for young people. What is your personal AGO in going to school?

6. There is a scare that certain cans of food from a particular manufacturer contain some harmful substances. This has not been proved. If you were the maker of those cans what would your AGO be?

7. In the back of a taxi you find an expensive camera. You are not sure if the cab driver has noticed you finding the camera. What should your AGO be?

8. Every government is concerned with the security of that country. There are different opinions on how this is best managed. If you were asked how you saw the AGO of the defence department, what would you suggest?

9. Do an AGO on the purpose of school tests.

FIP: First Important Priorities

This attention-directing tool is pronounced 'fipp'.

Many of the attention-directing tools are designed to broaden perception (CAF, C&S, OPV, PMI, APC). This is part of 'parallel' thinking: what else? We try to add to the list just as we try to think of more factors in CAF. With FIP as with AGO we try to narrow things down.

FIP is concerned directly with priorities. Forget about 'first important' as this is only put there to make 'FIP' pronounceable. With FIP we direct attention to priorities.

What are the priorities here?

Not everything is of equal importance. Some things are much more important than others. Some values are much more important than others.

... 'There are a lot of things that are important but which are the most important – we must do a FIP.'

... 'Before you can make a decision you need to know your priorities. Do a FIP.'

... 'I suspect my priorities are different from yours. Let us both do a FIP and then compare the outcome.'

The FIP tool is related to the AGO tool and also to focus and purpose, because just as we need to know our objective at the beginning so we also need to know our priorities.

The objective is what we are trying to reach. The priorities are the guidelines which tell us how we get there. Priorities are things that have to be taken into account. These are usually priority values and priority factors.

INCLUDE AND AVOID

Some priorities have to be included. Safety is a priority that has to be included in any thinking on aeroplanes and air traffic. Human rights and justice are priorities that have to be included in law and police matters. Ease of manufacture is usually a priority that has to be included by designers. Cost is a factor that has usually to be included in setting up any business – so are profits.

Some priorities have to be avoided. We should try to avoid pollution. We should try to avoid sharp edges and detachable pieces in toys for young children. We should try to avoid fear in medical care. We should make it difficult to cheat systems (fraud). We try to reduce risk.

Through language we can sometimes convert one type of priority into another: we should seek hygiene in food retailing; we should avoid food contamination. We should seek efficiency in energy use; we should avoid energy waste.

HOW MANY PRIORITIES?

When you look at a list of factors (for example in choosing a holiday) you might find that all of the factors seem to be priorities. Usually a case can be made for the importance and value of most things – if we try hard enough. But the point of FIP is to force us to make choices: what are the really important things (not what would we like to have).

So it is useful when doing a FIP exercise to set an artificial limit on the priorities. This limit could be three, four or five. You cannot go beyond these. You may be able to condense several factors or values into one priority.

In serious matters you need not stick to this artificial limit, but such a limit provides good thinking discipline.

EXERCISES ON FIP

1. If you were selecting people to be good police officers, what would your top three priorities be? Do a FIP.

2. If parents were able to select the characteristics of their children, what do you think the four top priorities of most parents would be? Do a FIP.

3. When a child has done something wrong, what would the three priorities of the parents be? Do a FIP.

4. In choosing a career, what would your four top priorities be? Do a FIP.

5. If you were going to elect someone to be leader of your group, what would you look for? Do a FIP on this (four priorities).

6. A businessman is choosing a salesman to go out and sell a new line of children's toys. He does a FIP and decides that the priorities he needs are:
energy and stamina
honesty
understanding of the toy market
clean appearance
Has anything been left out? If you were to do a FIP (only four priorities allowed) what would your FIP be?

7. There is an argument between parents and their children over what time the youngsters should be back home in the evening (choose ages of the youngsters as you wish). Do a FIP (three priorities) for the parents. Do a FIP (three priorities) for the children.

8. Do a FIP on choosing a friend.

9. Do a FIP on buying music tapes (or CDs).

First Review Section

At this point some readers of the book may be confused, so it is time to review what has been learned so far.

The most important thing to remember is that every one of the tools and habits that have been covered so far can be used entirely on its own. There is not some over-all structure in which everything has its place. Later on we shall come to some structures, but at this moment everything can be considered to be independent and able to stand on its own.

For example the black hat can be used on its own.

For example the OPV tool can be used on its own.

For example the C&S tool can be used on its own.

For example the 'values habit' can be used on its own.

For example the red hat can be used on its own.

For example the 'focus and purpose habit' can be used on its own.

I emphasize this because it is different from many other approaches to thinking. Many such approaches have complicated structures which look impressive but are very impractical in real life.

The famous Swiss Army penknife has many blades, each with a different function. You use the blades one at a time as appropriate: one blade is for cutting; another blade is a screwdriver; another blade opens bottles etc. Think again of the carpenter model I described as a basis for my approach to teaching thinking. The carpenter uses the hammer when he or she wants to use the hammer. There is no set structure.

I know, from many years of experience, that some youngsters will only remember one or two things: perhaps the PMI and CAF. Others might remember some of the hats (not all). Someone else might just remember the 'values habit' and perhaps the OPV. Even if someone just remembers the C&S that could be most useful.

Those who may be confused at this stage are those who are trying too hard to put everything together into one structure. Do not try to do this or you will end up confusing both yourself and whomever you are teaching.

TOOLS AND HABITS

I have covered a number of tools and habits. What is the difference between a tool and a habit?

HABIT: A habit is a routine that should always be present at the back of our minds no matter what we are thinking about. When you take a photograph you always need to be aware of: the focus, the shutter speed, the aperture, the film speed etc. These are things every professional photographer has to keep in mind. A habit is the same. Every skilled thinker keeps these habits in mind.

Each habit is framed as a question (or two questions) which the thinker is supposed to be asking himself or herself at frequent intervals. Only a few people will remember all the habits. Some people will remember one or two. Nevertheless all the habits are important and come into thinking at every stage. If you watch a good thinker you can observe how these background habits are always there.

TOOLS: A tool is more deliberate and more formal than a habit. You pick up a specific tool and you use it. Then you put it down again. Unlike habits, tools are not in use the whole time. Tools can give rise to habits. For example the OPV tool may encourage thinkers always to think of the other people affected by the thinking. Nevertheless, the OPV tool is a specific tool.

We need to be specific, formal and even artificial about the tools. We must say, 'Let's do a PMI', or, 'I want you to do a C&S on this.' The more formal and deliberate we are in the practice of these tools the more valuable they become as tools. As tools they are instructions that we give ourselves.

With habits, we just have to hope that frequent reminders will mean that the habits are used. With tools, we can have formal practice and we can request the use of a tool.

Very often when we are using a tool there are habits which go with the tool. For example the OPV tool automatically includes the value habit. All tools involve both the focus and outcome habit. The APC tool can call for changes in perception. And so on.

THE THINKING HABITS

I shall review here the thinking habits that have been covered so far in this book. They will be presented here not in the order in which they were learned but in a more logical order.

Focus and Purpose:

What am I looking at (thinking about) right now?

What am I trying to do?

This is a fundamental habit in the discipline of thinking. Without this habit there is drift, confusion and inefficiency. It is not enough to have a general notion of the subject of the thinking.

Forward and Parallel:

What else might there be?

So what follows?

This thinking habit determines the next step in thinking. Are we going to move forward from where we are, or are we going to move sideways (parallel) to consider possibilities? This choice can become a routine quite easily, particularly if we get into the habit of stopping now and again to ask: 'What else might there be?'

Perception and Logic:

How broad a view am I taking?

In what other ways is it possible to look at things?

The two important aspects of perception are breadth and change. As part of our thinking we always need to be aware of the importance of perception. I have not so far put down a question for logic because I shall be dealing with logic later. A simple question might be:

What follows from this?

This is very similar to the 'forward' question.

Values:

What are the values involved?

Who are affected by these values?

In all real-life thinking the values habit is essential. Quite simply, the values habit determines the whole value of the thinking (in real life). Without values there is no value to the thinking. It is quite obvious that the values habit needs to be a routine part of all thinking. The tragedy is that in a lot of school thinking there are abstract puzzles and mathematics problems in which this values aspect is not important. In real life values determine choices, decisions, success and failure.

Outcome and Conclusions:

If you have not succeeded in reaching a conclusion:

What have I found out?

What is the sticking point?

If you have reached a conclusion:

What is my answer?

Why do I think my answer will work?

Naturally, the 'outcome and conclusion' habit comes at the end of the thinking. It is an important habit for two reasons. The first reason is that if we have made a thinking effort we do want to 'harvest' the maximum we can from that effort – otherwise we have wasted our time. The second reason is that a sense of achievement in thinking is very important for motivation. Without achievement there is no motivation.

Summary:

Further thinking habits will be introduced later in the book. The habits introduced so far are fundamental in their nature and should be part of all thinking skill.

THE SIX THINKING HATS

The six thinking hats are somewhere between a tool and a structure for thinking. I have treated them as an attention-directing tool because they direct attention to a 'type' or mode of thinking.

The hats can be used individually and separately (occasional use) or in a sequence (systematic use).

WHITE HAT: Information, data, facts and figures. What information do we have? What information do we not have? How can we get this needed information? There is a relationship to CAF, OPV and possibly FIP.

RED HAT: Intuition, hunches, feelings and emotions. A legitimate way to put forward intuition and feelings and to label them as such. Relationship with values and OPV.

BLACK HAT: The hat of assessment and checking. Does what is suggested fit with our experience, our information, the systems, the values etc.? The black hat must always be logical and reasons must be given. Relationship to PMI and C&S.

YELLOW HAT: The benefits and the advantages of what is proposed. The reasons why something can work. Relationship to C&S and PMI. Like the black hat, must be logical.

GREEN HAT: Creativity, action, proposals and suggestions. This is the generative hat. Constructive ideas and new ideas. Direct relationship to APC.

BLUE HAT: Overview and control of the thinking process itself. What are we doing? What should we do next? Direct relationship to AGO, focus and purpose, outcome and conclusion.

The hats operate at a much more general level than the perceptual thinking tools. There is no great advantage in integrating the hats with the other tools.

THE THINKING TOOLS

The seven attention-directing thinking tools described so far are all taken from the full CoRT Thinking Program which is designed for use in education and is widely used in many schools. In that program there are sixty thinking lessons divided into sets of ten. Many further tools are covered.

The tools all have some acronym and the pronunciation of each acronym has been given. This acronym is important and is not just jargon – it is necessary in order to turn an attitude into a usable tool. It is important that the tools should be used explicitly, formally and deliberately. This can be done as a request or as an intention.

... 'I want you to do an OPV.'

... 'First of all I am going to do an AGO.'

The tools are reviewed here in the chronological order of use – not in the teaching order in which they have been presented in the book.

AGO: Aims, Goals and Objectives:

What is the objective of the thinking? What do we want to achieve? What do we want to end up with? The AGO directs attention to the specific purpose of the thinking. If we know exactly where we want to go we are more likely to get there.

CAF: Consider All Factors:

Look around. Explore. What factors should be considered in our thinking. Have we left out anything? What else should be considered? Before going ahead with the 'forward' thinking let us be sure attention has been paid to all those things which our thinking should take into account. We have to find the factors ourselves – they are not presented to us as they are in school textbooks. Real-life thinking can be a messy business. If you leave out important factors your thinking will never be any good.

OPV: Other People's Views:

People are doing the thinking and other people are going to be affected by the thinking. Let us use the OPV to pay direct attention to all these other people. Who are these people? What are the views of these people? What values are involved? There are the people who are directly involved or affected by the action that might result from the thinking. Then there are those who will be affected indirectly. Should the thinker take these other people into account or just look after his or her own values? Good thinking includes the frequent use of the OPV tool.

APC: Alternatives, Possibilities and Choices:

What are the alternative courses of action? What can be done? What are the possible solutions? It is with the APC that we set out to generate possible lines of action. APC also applies to explanations and perceptions. With the APC we search through our store of possible alternatives. What choices do we have? If we have no alternatives then we pause and try to construct an alternative.

FIP: First Important Priorities:

With the FIP tool we try to see what really matters. Not everything is equally important. When we have a clear view of the priorities, we can choose between the various alternatives. Which alternative best matches the priorities? Although the priorities are used at this stage of choosing between alternatives, the priorities may have been set up right at the beginning of the thinking after the AGO has been done. The more strict you are about priorities the easier decisions become.

C&S: Consequence and Sequel:

If we have chosen one alternative as a possible outcome of the thinking, let us see what would happen if we went ahead with the alternative. What would follow? What would the results be? The C&S can also be applied at the decision stage. By doing a C&S on each alternative we can see which is the best. The C&S, FIP and the PMI are all tools to help choosing between alternatives in decisions and in problem-solving (also in design). The C&S can be applied directly on its own to any suggested action or initiative.

PMI: Plus, Minus and Interesting:

A simple, attention-directing scan. Instead of just backing up our first judgement we explore the subject before coming to a decision. We can also use the PMI as an assessment of any conclusion, decisions or problem solution. We can also use the PMI to help us choose between alternatives by applying it to each available alternative. The 'interesting' part of the PMI scan opens up possibilities and speculations and leads on to creative thinking.

USE OF THE TOOLS

The order of the tools given here could be an order for the systematic use of the tools in thinking about some subject. Nevertheless, the main use of the tools is as independent tools. They can be used singly or as small groups of two or three. Just as a carpenter has to decide the most appropriate tool on any occasion so the thinker makes the same sort of choice. If people are involved, an OPV is important. If a reaction to a suggestion is necessary, a C&S or PMI is important. If a decision is needed, a CAF and a FIP are required. If a plan of action is needed, an AGO is most useful.

Because the tools are designed to be practical they often overlap. There are times when a PMI and a C&S may achieve the same thing. There are times when a CAF might include all the people who would be found with an OPV. A carpenter may use a hammer and nails or screws and a screwdriver to stick two pieces of wood together.

A thinker decides which tool to use and then uses it.

HABITS AND TOOLS

As I have mentioned the tools may lead to thinking habits. For example the APC leads to the habit of parallel thinking. The OPV leads to the habit of finding the values.

The other way around, the habits are useful when using the tools. For example focus and purpose help us to focus on the tool that is being used. After using the tool we need to assess the 'outcome': what have we achieved. With the use of many tools (CAF, OPV, C&S, PMI, FIP) we need to be aware of values the whole time.

SUMMARY

A number of thinking habits and thinking tools have been introduced. They can be used independently or in groups. They need to be practised as part of the skill of thinking.

REVIEW EXERCISES

1 Which single tool is most suitable for the following situations?
... you cannot find an important document that you need
... there is a fire in the kitchen
... there is a family disagreement over the housework
... the car breaks down on the highway.

2. A manager of a motel has some difficulties:
... a power failure
... a car belonging to a guest is stolen
... there is no bed long enough for a tall guest
... due to a mistake too many people have bookings
Which three of the following tools would be most use in each case:
OPV, APC, FIP, CAF or AGO?

3. There is a terrible smell coming from a locked garage. The owner is away. What thinking approach would you use?

4. Your aunt dies and leaves you an old house which is supposed to be haunted. What are you going to do? Suggest a thinking approach to this matter.

5. As part of a fund-raising carnival you are setting the rules for a 'laziness' competition. Which tools are likely to help you?

6. A friend of yours is very fat but cannot stop eating. Your help is asked. What thinking sequence would you use in your discussions with that friend?

7. Someone wants to open a hostel for homeless people in the neighbourhood. Everyone objects to this. A meeting is called. How should the thinking at the meeting be organized?

8. A comedian finds that people are not laughing at his jokes any more. What thinking tools should that comedian use?

9. You find that, by mistake, you have taken something from a store without paying. Use one thinking tool.

PART THREE

Broad and Detail

... 'What is the broad idea here?'

... 'For action we need the detailed idea.'

Have you ever 'travelled' along a road? Many times. In fact there has always been a 'detailed' way in which you have gone along any road: car, coach, motor-cycle, bicycle, on foot, on horse etc. 'Travel' is the broad idea or general method and then there is the detailed idea on how the method is actually put into practice.

Moving from broad idea to detailed idea and back again is both an important thinking habit and an important thinking operation.

... 'Get me a drink.'

... 'Get me a soft drink.'

... 'Get me a lemonade.'

We move from the broad to the detailed. In this case there are three levels. The detail level is always the one we can carry out. If any soft drink would do, that would be the detail level.

... 'I am going to reward him.'

... 'I am going to give him some money as a reward.'

... 'I am going to give him $50 as a reward.'

Again we move from the broad intention to the actual detail of what is to be done.

In much of our thinking we do have to be detailed and specific and sometimes being 'broad' means being unable to give a detailed answer. But there are other times when it is very useful to be able to work at the 'broad' level.

GENERATING ALTERNATIVES

In a concrete floor there is a hole that is filled with water. You want to get the water out of the hole.

... 'I could suck the water out.'

... 'I could lift the water out.'

... 'I could displace the water.'

Each of these is a broad idea, a general method or a broad concept. Once we have the broad idea we then go on to see in what ways that broad idea could be carried out as a detailed idea. 'Suck the water out' suggests a pump or a siphon. 'Lift the water out' suggests a small bucket, spoon, sponge or mop. 'Displace the water' suggests putting in stones or even a plastic bag filled with water and then removing these objects later.

Instead of immediately trying to find the detailed idea it is often more useful to define some broad ideas. Once you have the broad idea, you look around for actual ways of carrying it out in a detailed way.

It is very useful to get into the thinking habit of finding broad approaches to a matter or problem and then trying to work from these to specific details.

Generating ideas under the green hat or for an APC often needs to be done in this way.

EXTRACTING THE BROAD IDEA

Sometimes we start the other way round. Instead of setting out with a broad idea and then trying to find a detailed way of carrying out the idea, we can start with the detail and try to extract the broad idea that lies behind the detail.

A farmer has a pointed wooden stick that he jabs into the ground and then he drops a seed into the hole. What is the broad idea here? It could be: 'Making holes to put seeds into'. Or, it could be: 'Placing the seeds below the ground'.

Once we have the broad idea, we can look around for other ways to do things. For example, we could invent a machine that might make several holes at once and automatically drop a seed in each. Or we might scatter the seeds over the surface of the ground and then put a layer of soil on top of them.

If we are seeking to improve or change something, the way we do it is to extract the broad idea. Once we have the broad idea we can do two things. We can see if a different broad idea may serve the purpose (what we want to achieve). Or, we can see if the broad idea can be carried out in a different and better way.

What are we trying to do?

What is the broad idea here?

Is there a better broad idea?

How else can we carry out the broad idea?

CONCEPT AND FUNCTION

We often use a lot of different words to describe the 'broad idea'.
broad idea
general method
principle
broad concept
concept
function

In some cases it is more appropriate to use one word rather than another.

... 'What is the function of this switch?'

... 'The concept in this course is teach-yourself.'

... 'The principle is that of paying people by what they actually produce, not by time.'

... 'The general method we use here is to separate casualties into three groups: those who can wait; those who cannot be saved; those who need urgent attention.'

You should be aware of these different words. They do have slightly different meanings, but you would only confuse yourself by trying to remember the distinctions. Just think in terms of broad idea and detailed idea.

Often it is convenient to work at three levels: detailed idea, broad idea, broad approach. Really there are detailed ideas (which can be carried out) and then broad ideas. Some broad ideas are broader than others just as some roads are broader than others.

SUMMARY

It is useful to be able to work at the level of both broad idea and detailed idea. Moving up and down between these levels is an important thinking operation and a useful habit.

EXERCISES ON BROAD AND DETAIL

1. How would you describe the broad idea behind each of the following things?
traffic lights
a map
a car steering wheel
a parking lot

2. You have an interesting new hobby, or a new friend, and you want to spend as much time as possible on that hobby or with the new friend. Give two broad approaches to how you might find the time.

3. A dog feels that she is being badly treated in a particular household. What broad action ideas could that dog have?

4. A caterer is in the middle of preparing food for a large party when there is a telephone call threatening to put poison in the food unless some protection money is paid. What are his broad action options?

5. At a supermarket there are always long lines at the check-out counter. You want to improve this situation. What is the broad idea that is being used? Can you think of a better way of carrying out that broad idea?

6. You are invited to a fancy-dress party. Give three broad ideas regarding possible choice of costume (not details).

7. Your brother (or sister or friend) is always taking your things without telling you. This can be irritating. What broad approaches to this problem can you find?

8. A politician knows that he does not look good on television. What can he do about this? (Two broad ideas.)

9. What is the broad idea behind sport?

Basic Thinking Operations

There are many sets of muscles in the human hand. There are muscles for closing the fingers and for extending the fingers. When we use the hand for anything useful we always use combinations of the muscles. So although the basic actions of the different muscle groups can be identified and described, this is of more value for description than for action. It would not be too much use just exercising the different muscle groups and hoping that this would give us a skilled use of the hand. It is far better to exercise the muscles in combination.

It is somewhat the same with basic thinking operations. These do exist and they can be described. But whenever we use thinking in real life we nearly always use combinations of these basic operations. It is better to practise these combinations than to practise the basic operations. This is the difference between philosophical description and practical operacy.

This is the reason why I have not dealt with the basic operations until now. It was far more important to acquire some practical thinking habits and tools that could actually be used. At this point, however, there is some value in considering the basic operations, because understanding the basic operations may help us to use the thinking tools more effectively.

CARPENTER MODEL

Early in this book I put forward the carpenter model for the skilled thinker. I mentioned that the carpenter has three basic operations: cutting, sticking and shaping. I know that there are actually some further operations but these three are fundamental. I am going to take the model of those three basic operations and apply it to the basic operations of thinking. Although the fit is not exact, the simplicity of the model has advantages.

THE CUTTING OPERATION

You cut a piece of wood, you cut a piece of cake, you cut a slice of water melon. 'Cutting' means that you do not want the whole thing. You want to remove part of the whole.

When we direct attention to part of the world around us we are 'cutting' a piece out of the whole. So all attention directing is a form of cutting.

FOCUS: We direct attention to part of the whole. We may eventually pay attention to the whole but do it bit by bit. We may also move in and out from a close-up view to a long-distance view – from a view of detail to a view of the whole.

EXTRACT A FEATURE: From the whole situation we pull out or extract a feature. This is a much-used operation in thinking and is the basis of other operations. For example in the operations of 'movement' (which we shall come to later as part of lateral thinking) we extract one feature of a provocation and then move forward to see where it can take us. When we extract a concept or principle we are pulling out a relationship.

ANALYSIS: When we extract a feature we can leave the rest behind. With analysis, however, we seek to be comprehensive. There should be no left-overs. We seek to break down the situation into parts or pieces. These parts and their relationship describe the whole situation.

EXPANSION: In the diagram overleaf there is a drawing of a square. You could pay attention to the whole square. Or, you could pay attention to just a corner of the square. When we pay attention to the whole square we are really cutting that square out of its surroundings. Expansion means taking a bigger cut which includes not only the square but more of its surroundings. Though 'expansion' seems to be the opposite of 'cutting' this is not really the case. The mind is just taking a bigger view of the surroundings.

In a restaurant you are served a grilled trout and some fried potatoes on a plate. As the plate is served you pay attention to the whole plate. As you eat you pay attention to the fish or part of the fish or a single chip. But you could sit back and pay attention to the whole table (your eating companions) or you could pay attention to the

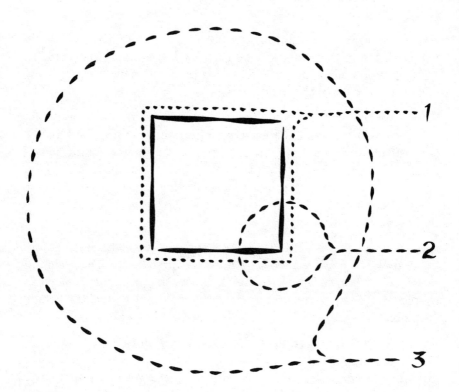

whole restaurant (the décor, the other diners etc.). The attention area can get smaller or bigger. The obvious attention area with which we are presented is only one size of cut.

So expansion and exploration are actually part of the 'cutting' process of thinking. Think of a wide-angle lens on a camera. This takes a bigger picture.

THE STICKING OPERATION

The sticking operation is where things are put together and they do not just fall apart. If you put two random things together for no reason at all and no connection develops between them, they remain 'unstuck'. Placing two pieces of wood together is not sticking the pieces together. For that there must be some sort of attachment or glue.

CONNECTIONS: The mind is very good at making connections. These may just be associations. Things have occurred together in space or time, so there is an association. Sometimes the link is stronger and there is a functional connection. If we place things together in a group or category, there is a linking factor (or factors) which all members of the group possess. Whenever we consider anything there are 'tentacles' which spread out in our mind from that thing. These tentacles make connections. The larger the number of tentacles the greater the chance of a connection. The greater our experience the larger the number of tentacles (or potential connectors).

RECOGNITION: This is a fundamental thinking operation that arises directly from connection. What is before our eyes (or ears etc.) connects up with a pattern we already have stored in our mind. So we recognize the object and know what to do with it.

A slight pressure on a trigger can fire a mighty gun. In the same way something small may trigger an important pattern in the mind. For example, 'death' is a small word written on this page, but the image it triggers is powerful. Those who are particularly interested in how the mind forms and uses patterns should read my book *I Am Right – You Are Wrong*,* in which I describe how self-organizing systems allow patterns to form.

*Penguin Books, Harmondsworth, 1991

Pattern recognition and extrapolation into the future are based on a combination of recognition and checking.

SYNTHESIS: This is where we deliberately put things together to produce an effect. Writing any sentence is an example of synthesis. Combination of any sort is a form of synthesis (which was originally supposed to be a combination of thesis and anti-thesis).

CONSTRUCTION: This could be regarded as being the same as synthesis but I prefer 'construction' as this has a broader meaning. Synthesis suggests putting together what is now present. Construction may imply building things up step by step.

DESIGN: This is a form of construction. Things are put together in a certain way to achieve a defined objective. In design there are elements of creativity and, sometimes, aesthetics.

In general the 'sticking operation' consists of two things:

1. Recognizing connections that are there.

2. Putting things together for a purpose.

THE SHAPING OPERATION

The carpenter has a shape in mind. The carpenter may even have that shape drawn up on a piece of cardboard (a template). As the carpenter shapes with the plane he or she continually checks the emerging shape against the planned shape.

It is this constant checking between the desired shape and the actual shape that is the basis of the thinking operation of shaping. In fact the operation could be called 'checking'.

JUDGEMENT: Is this correct? Does this fit what I know? Does this fit the facts? These are all aspects of black-hat checking. There is something against which we are checking or judging what is placed before us. Is that really a painting by Rubens? Let us check various characteristics.

In real life, 'assessing' is often a complex form of both exploration and judgement. We explore the effects of a planned action both now and into the future. We then judge those effects against norms. If our exploration suggests that use of a certain farm fertilizer is going to give river pollution, then pollution (judged against no pollution) is not desirable.

MATCHING: Here we set out with specific needs and then check to see whether what we find matches those needs. Whenever you ask a question you are setting up a need for information. When you are given an answer you check whether the answer matches your needs. If an engineer is searching for a material with certain characteristics, he checks all possibilities to see if any known material has these characteristics. If he makes up new materials, he checks these too.

HYPOTHESIS: Usually we check what we find against something that we already know (laws, facts etc.). With a hypothesis we imagine a possible mechanism (or explanation) and then see how well evidence supports that hypothesis. In speculation (what if ...?) we do the same. We throw up tentative and even provocative ideas and then seek to check them out. Scientific thinking includes the ability both to set up such hypotheses and also to check them out.

COMPARISON: Often in judgement or checking we compare something in front of us with something we have in mind. For example recognition is always followed by checking: is this really what I believe it to be? A doctor thinks he recognizes an illness, forms a hypothesis and then checks by X-rays and other tests.

With comparison we may have two (or more) things in front of us and we set about comparing them. In essence this means looking for points of similarity and points of difference.

It is sometimes said that scientists are divided into 'lumpers' and 'splitters'. The lumper notices that things which seem very different actually have things in common, so they get lumped together (with valuable results). The splitter notices that things which seem the same actually have important points of difference, so he makes distinctions and splits them apart (also with valuable results). In general, how we deal with the world as children or as a society is a matter of lumping and splitting. That is how we form concepts in the first place and then go on to form better concepts.

SUMMARY

We can identify some basic thinking operations. These can be grouped under three types: cutting, sticking and shaping. Usually thinking involves combinations of these basic operations. For example even the simple behaviour of picking the odd man out in a group involves attention directing, concept extraction, hypothesis forming and checking. An understanding of these basic operations helps the development of thinking skills. But practice at these basic operations is insufficient to develop thinking skills.

EXERCISES ON BASIC THINKING OPERATIONS

1. Analyse the following items into their parts: ladder, kitchen, school, money.

2. Extract two important features from each of the following items: roof, bus, newspaper, sneeze.

3. For every word in the first column find as many connections as possible to each word in the second column.

mouse	bucket
sign	cheese
food	pen
cow	horse
train	computer

4. See in how many ways you can group the following eight items into two groups of four items each: soldier, frog, river, cloud, car, hammer, wine, virus.

5. Each of the following sets of three features describes one or more specific items. See how many items you can match with each set of features.
dangerous, sharp, no handle
animals, children, paper
two wheels, very long, noisy

6. Pick out and list the similarities and differences you can find between the items of each pair given below.
holiday / cake   bank / book   running / walking   children / adults

7. Create a hypothesis to explain these situations:
. . . the shops on one side of the high street do much better than the shops on the other side.
. . . many birds have bright colours.
. . . some countries drive on the right side, some on the left.

Truth, Logic and Critical Thinking

It is easy enough to describe and to define a lie. Someone asks you what your age is. You know it to be fourteen years old but you say sixteen years. That is a lie.

Unfortunately it is very much more difficult to define 'truth' except as the opposite of a lie.

When we are thinking or communicating, truth is important if we are not to make mistakes.

In practical terms there are two sorts of truth. There is 'game truth' and 'reality truth'.

GAME TRUTH: If you set up a game with rules and definitions, matters which agree with those rules and definitions are true and matters which do not agree are false. If you set up a game so that $2 + 2 = 4$, clearly the answer '5' is false. If someone wants to move a chess piece in a novel way, that is not allowed. Over the ages philosophers and others have tried very hard to set up language as a game truth. But where language deals with reality rather than an abstract created game, there are difficulties.

REALITY TRUTH: How true are our ideas and information to the actual real world? We rely on perceptions and imperfect knowledge. From time to time even scientists are convinced they are right – but find out they have been mistaken. Reality truth is very important for most practical thinking. Even with mathematics there is a stage in which our perceptions of the real world have to be translated into symbols.

We live in a practical world and we do have to get on with things. We have to make decisions and plan action. We cannot always wait for absolute truth. So there are different levels of practical 'reality truth' that we use.

1. Checkable truth. You can check something again and again and

always come up with the same answer. Other people can check it and will also get the same answer. It is quite possible that everyone's methods of checking (or instruments) are intrinsically faulty.

2. Personal experience. We tend to believe the evidence of our own eyes. But we can be mistaken. Memory may play tricks on us. There is illusion, deception and even hallucination.

3. Second-hand experience. What other people tell us. Even if another person is sincere and reliable, that person may have got the information from someone who is not so reliable. In any case people may be reliable and sincere and yet mistaken.

4. Generally accepted. It is part of the culture or accepted knowledge. The earth goes around the sun. Deficiency of vitamin C will cause scurvy. We only need to look back in history to see that over and again generally accepted ideas turn out to be false.

5. Authority. The authority of parents, teachers, reference books, scientists, religious leaders can provide a higher check on truth than is available to most people – so we tend to accept these matters. Again, history has shown us that authority can be mistaken. All the best medical authorities once believed that bleeding (leeches) was the best form of treatment for most illnesses. Mathematicians proved that it would be impossible to get a rocket to the moon or have man-powered flight. Religious authority is in a somewhat different position because here we partly move into constructed 'game truth' where something is true within the belief system.

Consider the following statements about cows.

. . . cows can fly.
This is contrary to our experience or anyone's experience. It is also contrary to our definition of a cow. We would dismiss the idea as ridiculous just as a biologist would at first have dismissed reports of the Australian duck-billed platypus.

. . . cows produce methane which pollutes the atmosphere.
Many people would not be in a position to question this point and would have to accept it on authority. Cows are said to release 70 million tonnes of methane into the atmosphere every year. This has a more powerful greenhouse effect than carbon dioxide (for equivalent amounts).

. . . cows rely on microbes to digest food for them.
Again a matter of knowledge or acceptance on authority.

... all cows have horns.

If your personal experience has always been with horned cows you might agree. If you have come across cows without horns you would not agree. The problem is with the word 'all'.

... cows give milk all the time.

A matter of experience or a knowledge of biology (even human biology). Cows give milk when they have had calves.

... cows are dangerous animals.

A matter of personal experience. Some cows might be dangerous but it is generally accepted that bulls are dangerous but cows are not.

... cows are colour-blind.

A matter of special knowledge. You might argue that since bulls seem to respond to the matador's red cape they might not be colour-blind. This is an inference.

... cows love to eat fish.

You have never heard it to be so. But it could be.

... cows are very efficient at converting grass into protein.

You would have to believe this until you could think of a more efficient way of making the conversion (there are more efficient ways).

... cows are sacred animals.

You might laugh at that idea because it is totally contrary to your own experience. But if you knew about India you would know that in the Hindu culture cows are indeed regarded as sacred. Here is an example of how something may be true in one circumstance and not true in another. This is an important point I shall come back to later.

THINKING HABIT

As part of our thinking habits we should always be asking the question:

What is the truth value here?

You then determine the truth value level, as in the examples about the cow. You need not accept everything you are told. You can try to check things (especially information) for yourself.

Perhaps the most important difficulty in thinking, particularly where other people are involved, is the 'claimed' truth value.

... 'This is so.'

... 'This is absolutely true.'

... 'This is always true.'

If that is the claim made for the truth value then you need to check the value very closely. On the other hand if the claim is more modest, you might accept it.

... 'This is sometimes the case.'

... 'I remember reading that.'

... 'This could be true.'

... 'Someone once told me.'

There is always the balance between the claimed truth value and the actual truth value.

Unfortunately in thinking and argument people tend to be dogmatic and certain in order to make their point.

Also, our normal everyday habits of logic often make us insist on words like 'all', 'always', 'never' because without these absolutes the logic would not work. If we were just to say 'by and large', 'in general', 'on the whole', 'in my experience', we would be closer to the truth but unable to use the power of inclusion/exclusion logic.

LOGIC

With logic we move from the present position to a new one. No new outside information is coming in. We work forward from what we have (deductive logic).

Our first examination of truth value was whether something corresponded with reality.

Our second examination of truth value is whether something follows from what we have (according to the line of argument).

Punishment deters people from crime.
Therefore if we want to decrease crime we must (could) use punishment.

First we need to look at the evidence for the claim that punishment deters people from crime. It is reasonable to suppose this but it may not be true (criminals do not expect to be caught).

If we accept this first claim, then we look at whether the conclusion follows. There is no justification for 'must', but punishment could be one option, so we might use 'could'. We would also need to look at the amount of punishment, the type of crime, the cost, the after-effects of punishment etc.

The habit questions to be asked are:

Does this follow?

Even more important is the question:

Must this follow (as claimed)?

A logical argument depends on something that must follow. If we are content 'it can' follow then that is a suggestion and an exploration (and useful as such).

LOGIC, INFORMATION AND CREATIVITY

We very often forget that the 'must follow' of a logical argument is actually based not on logic but on a lack of creativity or information.

A man enters a room in which there is a beautiful crystal vase. The room is sealed. No one can enter the room. There are no windows or apertures into the room. Ten minutes later the man comes out. The vase is found broken in the room. He denies breaking the vase. But surely he must have broken the vase – there is no other possible explanation.

We need creativity or information to think of the possibility of a high-pitched tone shattering the glass. Once we have such thoughts, we can no longer say he 'must' have done it. That is what a good criminal lawyer is all about.

People over-eat and become fat and unhealthy.
If we raised the price of food people would buy less food.
If people bought less food they would become more healthy.

We might accept the logic of this line of argument until our creativity suggested some alternative outcomes.

The people might buy just as much food but spend more money which they take from other spending areas.

The people might spend the same amount of money but buy cheaper junk food – which might in fact be more unhealthy.

In real-life situations apparently logical lines of argument are often (not always) based on an inability to see alternative possibilities.

In a similar way the ability to think of an alternative explanation is by far the best way of destroying the arrogance of an apparently logical line of argument.

We saw lights coming down into that field last night.
The air force say there is no record of any aircraft in that area last night.
Therefore it must have been a UFO.

It could have been a drug smuggler's plane flying low enough to avoid radar.

If you toss a coin on to a hard surface it is rather unlikely to stand on edge. So if it is not heads, it must be tails. Logic works best when there are only a limited number of possibilities. If all other possibilities have been excluded, it must be the remaining one. Unfortunately we are very apt to say there are only limited possibilities when these are limited only by our knowledge and our creative imagination.

By definition contradictory things cannot both exist. The difficulty is to decide whether two things really are contradictory. We have love–hate relationships and in Japan it is perfectly possible for someone to be friend and not-friend because the Japanese do not have the Western horror of contradictions.

On the whole the difficulties with logic arise when we are trying to describe the world as it is. When we are dealing with a constructed game, logic is much more powerful. The question then becomes: is language a constructed game or a description of our perceptions?

CRITICAL THINKING

If we use the term 'critical thinking' to mean all thinking, we do not need the term 'critical' and we also lose the specific meaning of the term 'critical'.

The word 'critical' comes from the Greek word for 'judge' and passes through the Latin. The dictionary definition (Oxford) suggests 'censorious' or fault-finding.

Often 'critical' is taken to mean an assessment, whether this is good or bad. This sense, however, weakens the main value of critical thinking.

The original purpose of critical thinking was to uncover the truth by attacking and removing all that was false – so the truth would be revealed. This has a considerable value in discouraging the sloppy use of language, concepts and false arguments, but it lacks generative and constructive power. This is the point I made much earlier in this book.

To be sure the removal of weaknesses – as in black-hat thinking – will strengthen an idea, but that is not enough for constructive thinking.

Critical thinking does have a value as does one wheel on a motorcar. But the teaching only of critical thinking is quite insufficient. Reactive thinking by itself is insufficient.

Water puts out fires.
Water is a liquid.
Gasoline is a liquid.
So gasoline should put out fires.

Critical thinking would point this out as a classic error of reasoning. John loves eating oysters. John is a boy. Peter is also a boy – so Peter must love eating oysters. We can easily see that this does not follow.

The reasoning might have gone differently.
All the liquids I have ever come across (water, mud, milk, urine) put out fire.
This may be due to their liquid nature which prevents air getting to the fire.
Gasoline is a new liquid (which I have not come across before) so it is reasonable to suppose it might put out a fire.

This line of inductive reasoning seems quite valid. It is only my experience with gasoline or knowledge about gasoline which tells me otherwise.

SUMMARY

Truth is very important for thinking. There is truth in constructed systems (games) and truth as it refers to the world around. Using our critical thinking we need to ask:

Is this true?

We seek to determine the practical level of truth.

We use logic to derive further truths from ones we have already. We need to check this logical truth with another question:

Must this follow from what we have?

EXERCISES ON TRUTH, LOGIC AND CRITICAL THINKING

1. 'If I give you half of what I have got it is only fair that you give me half of what you have got.' Is this logical? Does it follow?

2. We know that Ellen is very lazy – so we should give her extra work to make her work harder. Use your critical thinking on this.

3. The enemy of my enemy is my friend. Does this follow?

4. Assess the truth level of the following statements:
... yellow cars have least accidents.
... red cars are difficult to see at night.
... men drive better than women.
... women alone in a car drive fastest of all.
... men cause more accidents.
... at any level alcohol impairs driving.
... slow drivers can cause accidents.
... the front passenger seat is the most dangerous.
... wet roads provide a better grip for tyres.
... motor-cycles are only dangerous because riders are young.
... the top traffic light is the red one.

5. An office calculates that every letter sent costs $20 (space, secretarial time, postage etc.). To cut down costs they decide to send fewer letters. Is this logical?

6. These shoes are more expensive so the quality must be better. If

the quality were not better no one would buy them and the makers would have gone out of business. Does this follow?

7. 'When you cook the meals, then you can decide what you want to eat.' Use your critical thinking on this.

8. In a food store, theft is 3 per cent of turnover. Profits are only 2 per cent of turnover. Does it follow that the store will go out of business?

Under What Circumstances?

'There is something wrong with this thermometer. The reading won't go higher than 96 degrees but the water seems to be boiling. Shouldn't it read 100 degrees?'

Everyone knows that water boils at 100 degrees centigrade (212 degrees Fahrenheit). Right? Wrong. Water boils at 100°C only at sea-level. If the air pressure decreases as you go up a mountain, water boils at a lower temperature. So the scientific truth that water boils at 100°C holds only under special circumstances.

During a lecture I gave in Plovdiv, Bulgaria, a young psychologist who was sitting in front of me in the first row kept shaking her head vigorously at almost anything I said. I found this very disconcerting and after the talk asked her why she disagreed so strongly with what I had to say. She told me that a vigorous, side-to-side shake of the head in Bulgaria meant full agreement.

Everyone knows that cows are not sacred animals. But under the circumstances of the Hindu religion and culture in India cows are treated as sacred and if a cow chooses to sit in the middle of the busiest road the traffic just parts and drives around her.

It stands to reason that milk must be good for people, so relief organizations used to give milk to starving children during the war in Vietnam. The children got diarrhoea. Some people (particularly in South-East Asia) do not have the right enzyme – lactase – with which to digest the milk.

Salt is good. Salt makes food taste better. The human body needs salt. But too much salt on food tastes bad.

In all these examples something which seems to be obvious and true turns out to be true only under certain circumstances.

The science of chemistry depends very heavily on circumstances or conditions. Compounds will interact only under exactly the right circumstances of temperature or pressure or only in the presence of the right catalyst.

You could argue that when we are talking or thinking we take for granted the normal culture and conditions and that it is only under very special circumstances that things are no longer true. On the contrary, whenever we claim a truth we need to specify the circumstances under which the truth holds.

Perhaps the most common fault in argument or discussions is this failure to specify the circumstances. Often both parties to the disagreement are right – but under different circumstances.

Does this mean that all truth is relative? Not at all. It means that some truth is relative. All human beings require oxygen. We like to believe that all human beings have certain basic human rights. It is just that we have to be careful with those words 'all' and 'always' which are the foundation of our usual logic. We could say 'by and large' instead of 'always' but if we do want to say 'always' we need to define the circumstances.

There are some exceptions to most generalizations. I am not writing about those exceptions but about truths which hold under certain circumstances but not under other circumstances.

THINKING HABIT

We need to get into the thinking habit of asking an important question:

Under what circumstances is this true (does it apply)?

EXERCISES ON CIRCUMSTANCES

1. Under what circumstances would each of the following items be very useful? Can you then think of circumstances under which two or more of the items would be useful?
a piece of rope
a rubber balloon
a cigarette lighter
a bucket
an ice-cream

2. Are the following statements always true or are they true only under certain circumstances:

... icebergs are dangerous.

... wet hands are dangerous.

... careless driving is dangerous.

... dieting is dangerous.

... knives are dangerous.

... swimming pools are dangerous.

3. Which of the following things are good in reasonable amounts but not good if you have too much of them?

food

money

exercise

knowledge

honesty

sleep

television

4. A neighbour's guard dog has bitten a boy. The neighbour maintains that the dog is normally very quiet but that the boy was provoking the dog. The boy's parents say that the dog is vicious and must be removed. What do you think?

5. On the whole do you think people behave well or badly? Give the circumstances under which you think they behave well. Give the circumstances under which you think they behave badly.

6. Is fire dangerous or useful?

Hypothesis, Speculation and Provocation

Hypothesis, speculation and provocation are very important thinking skills for progress, change, science and creative thinking of any sort. Unfortunately most traditional approaches to thinking ignore these important matters.

Why do kittens play? Probably to try out behaviour patterns for hunting or for defence. Possibly because they are full of energy and fun.

Why do humans play? For fun and enjoyment. And also to try out new things.

Hypothesis, speculation and provocation allow us to play in our minds. We try out new things. We carry out the 'thought experiments' that Einstein used to generate his powerful ideas.

... 'Maybe we could breed very small cows – no bigger than dogs.'

... 'Suppose we made cows mature more quickly by using growth hormone.'

... 'What if we could put even more efficient microbes into a cow's digestive system so that grass could be converted into food more thoroughly?'

... 'Would it be possible to treat household garbage in such a way that it could be used for cattle feed?'

... 'Po cows could fly.' (Po is a new word – a deliberately provocative tool in lateral thinking, to be considered later.)

All these are examples of speculations and provocations.

JUMP AHEAD

In normal thinking there must be a reason for saying something before you say it.

As we move 'forward' with logical thinking we proceed from the present position to the next position: 'This follows on from what we now have.' This is the normal logical line of argument. It is shown in the diagram opposite where we move from A to B and then on to C. Where we are at any moment is determined by where we have been before. Each new position can be logically supported.

But there is another way of moving 'forward' in our thinking. This other way is to take a 'jump ahead'. This process is shown in the diagram opposite. Here we jump from A to D. Once we are at D we can 'pull' the next step forward from A.

The difference is between 'push' and 'pull'. In push thinking we push ahead from where we are – just as an ice-breaker pushes through the ice. In pull thinking we jump ahead and then see if we can find a path through the ice.

In push thinking we say:

'This is so – and as a result that follows.'

In pull thinking we say:

'This could be so and if we make this jump then that might follow.'

In normal logical thinking each step forward must be fully justified. When we jump ahead with speculation there is no full justification for the jump. With provocation there may not be a reason for saying something until after you have said it (the results of saying it justify the provocation).

LEVELS OF SPECULATION

In speculative thinking we use a number of different words:
... maybe
... suppose
... perhaps
... possibly

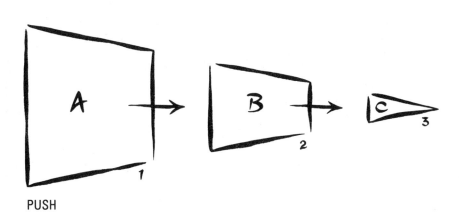

PUSH

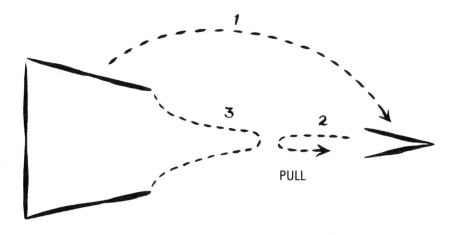

PULL

. . . what if
. . . po (described later)

The levels of certainty range from the full certainty of good logic to the deliberate provocation of lateral thinking.

CERTAIN: The result of good logical deduction.

REASONABLY SURE: Not yet absolutely certain but very likely indeed. Just needs final confirmation. Also anything to do with the future where absolute certainty is difficult.

GOOD GUESS: We know it is a guess but it is a good guess and certainly the best available guess.

POSSIBLE: This is no more than a possibility. There is not much supportive evidence but it is a possibility. Sometimes it is no more than 'just possible'.

TENTATIVE: This is 'flying a kite'. This is putting forward an idea that is not thought to be very reasonable to see what effect it has.

PROVOCATION: Here there is no claim at all for reasonableness or probability. A provocation is designed to get us out of our usual thinking. The provocation can be signalled with the word 'po', which indicates that it is indeed a provocation. 'Po cars should have square wheels.'

ACTION AND CHANGE

Doctors have to take practical action. Yet they rarely have all the information they require: because the tests are not yet through and because we know relatively little about the human body. So the action the doctor takes is based on things that are reasonably sure or the best guess.

In many practical cases action cannot be based on certainty but has to be based on reasonable speculation. But that is not the type of speculation that I am considering here.

In this section I am looking at speculation as a powerful tool for progress, for changing ideas, for forming new ideas and for creativity in general.

CREATIVE ATTITUDE

In argument and in much of thinking we want to confirm what we already know. With a creative attitude we want to move forward to something new.

Speculation allows us to open up new possibilities and then to pursue these possibilities.

Speculation allows us to set up new frames so that we can look at the evidence in a new way.

Speculation and provocation allow us to develop deliberate creative thinking tools to get us out of the traditional thinking patterns.

Without speculation we can get the steady development and improvement of an idea, but we are not likely to get a really new idea.

The creative attitude involves risk and play and trying things out.

SCIENTIFIC THINKING

The traditional scientific method is to collect and analyse the evidence. From this analysis comes the most reasonable hypothesis. Then we set out to check the hypothesis. In theory we should try hard to prove that hypothesis to be wrong. In practice many scientists try hard to prove the hypothesis to be right.

A lot of the emphasis in scientific training is on the collection and analysis of data. It has always been supposed that the analysis of data will produce the most reasonable hypothesis. Today many people are having serious doubts about that.

Does the analysis of data produce new ideas or does it allow us to confirm existing ideas? From what we know about the behaviour of the mind as a self-organizing system, it follows that the mind can only see what it is already prepared to see. So we have a stock of existing hypotheses through which we examine the data. This will not produce really new ideas.

This is why scientific breakthroughs (and what are called 'paradigm shifts') take so very long. Those who see the data through the old idea are very slow to move to the new idea.

The analysis of data by itself is not enough. We also need the creative ability to speculate and to use provocative hypotheses. If we can develop these skills in scientists, science will advance more rapidly.

The new hypothesis or provocative idea provides a scaffold on which to organize our information and with which to seek new information.

These new hypotheses are not limited to the 'most reasonable'. They can be deliberately speculative and provocative.

BUSINESS THINKING

New initiatives, new ventures, new enterprises are all examples of speculative thinking. The idea is put together and then we seek to check it out through collecting information and doing market research. There may still be an element of risk – even though the entrepreneur is convinced that he or she is logically correct.

In launching new products or new strategies there is always speculative thinking: 'What if we do this . . .?' The response of competitors has to be guessed at.

Because business is always dealing with action and with the future there is always speculation. Should we then not try to reduce the amount of speculation rather than to increase it? We need to do both at the same time. We need to reduce speculation and risk by collecting information, using monitoring and having back-up strategies. At the same time we need to increase the speculation in terms of new ventures and new directions and new methods.

SUMMARY

In much of our thinking we make a logically justified step forward from our present position to the next position. With hypothesis, speculation and provocation we may make a jump ahead which is not fully justified. The degree of justification may range from a reasonable guess to an outright provocation with no justification.

The value of hypothesis, speculation and provocation is that they allow us to play around, to try new ideas and to see things in a new way. In any self-organizing information system (like the mind) there is a logical necessity for this behaviour.

EXERCISES ON HYPOTHESIS, SPECULATION AND PROVOCATION

1. Why do you think mice have tails? Put forward two different hypotheses.

2. The family has gone away for the weekend. When you all come back there is a very bad smell in the kitchen. What do you think it might be?

3. In many fairy stories a person is granted three wishes by some djinn who has been rescued from a bottle. Suppose you were to be granted three wishes. What would these wishes be? What would happen if each were to be granted?

4. A manager notices that an assistant who has always been very punctual in the mornings has started to arrive later at work. What are the possible explanations? Give two very reasonable explanations. Give two explanations which are 'just possible' but unlikely.

5. Someone you know has always been scruffy and untidy and lazy. Suddenly this person starts to dress neatly, is very tidy and organized and begins to work hard. Speculate on what you think might have happened.

6. A business manager finds that his main competitor seems to know ahead of time what is going to happen. The manager suspects a leak. The situation is as follows:
. . . a senior assistant left three months before.
. . . the assistant was replaced by someone on the recommendation of a friend.
. . . false information given to the new assistant is not used by the competitor.
. . . the assistant who left is working in another part of the country.
What do you think is going on?

7. Why do you think people like to argue? Try to provide three different hypotheses.

8. Suppose cows were very small. What would happen?

Lateral Thinking

Is creativity a mysterious talent possessed by a few people?

Is creative thinking a part of the skill of thinking and therefore a skill that can be learned and developed?

CREATING: The word 'creative' in the English language can mean making something or bringing something about. What is made is new because it was not there before. But there may be no new ideas involved. I prefer to call this 'constructive' thinking.

ART: The word 'creative' is very broad and covers art because in art new things are produced. Art includes powers of expression, emotional resonance and many other things. Some artists (in music, design, architecture, drama etc.) have told me that they do use my methods – but I am not claiming to be talking about artistic creativity.

GENIUS: I do not guarantee to make everyone a genius. The genius level of creativity may indeed depend on special qualities (such as an ability to image) just as the idiot savants seem to possess special abilities. Nevertheless, many geniuses have used methods that relate to lateral thinking. For example, Einstein's 'thought experiments' were classic examples of provocation.

CHANGING IDEAS AND PERCEPTIONS: I am specifically concerned with the ability to change ideas and perceptions. This is the purpose of lateral thinking.

If lateral thinking is indeed a skill, everyone can acquire some skill in lateral thinking if he or she puts in the effort.

As with any skill, some people will become much more skilful than others.

Over the years many people who are naturally creative and have achieved creative success have told me that they find the techniques and disciplines of lateral thinking very helpful.

ORIGIN

I invented the term 'lateral thinking' in 1967. The term is now
officially part of the English language, with an entry and attribution
in the *Oxford English Dictionary*.

From time to time people have always used lateral thinking in the
sense of coming up with new perceptions and new ideas. From time
to time random experiences have triggered new ideas.

My contribution has been to identify this as a valid and valuable
part of thinking, to formalize it, to develop techniques that can
be used deliberately and – above all – to relate lateral thinking to
self-organizing information systems. If we look at the behaviour of
self-organizing information systems we see that there is a logical and
mathematical necessity for lateral thinking. It is not a luxury.

USE OF LATERAL THINKING

Anyone who has to do any thinking at all needs to acquire some
skill in lateral thinking. It is not something that is restricted to
architects, advertisers, new-product designers and inventors.

All thinking is a combination of perception and logic. Lateral thinking is essential in perceptual thinking.

DEFINITION

There are different levels of definition.

'You cannot dig a hole in a different place by digging the same hole
deeper.'

Trying harder with the same ideas and the same approach may not
solve the problem. You may need to move 'laterally' to try new ideas
and a new approach.

'Lateral thinking is for escaping from established ideas and perceptions in order to find new ones.'

Our existing ideas have been established by particular sequences of
experience. We tend to defend the established ideas and to see the

world through the established perceptions. Lateral thinking is a means of escaping from the existing ideas and perceptions in order to find better ones.

'A self-organizing information system allows incoming information to organize itself into patterns. These patterns are not symmetric. We need a means for cutting across patterns (moving laterally). Lateral thinking provides that means.'

Obviously this is a technical definition and will not mean much to those who do not understand what is meant by a self-organizing system. This is the technical definition of lateral thinking and indicates that it is more than just a descriptive term. Lateral thinking is based on information behaviour in self-organizing systems.

GENERAL AND SPECIFIC

The specific meaning of 'lateral thinking' covers the use of specific techniques which are used to help us generate new ideas and new perceptions. This is directly concerned with creative thinking.

The general meaning of 'lateral thinking' covers thinking that sets out to explore and to develop new perceptions instead of just working harder with the existing perceptions. In this sense lateral thinking is closely connected with perceptual thinking. Many of the attention directing tools (CAF, OPV, C&S) are part of this general exploration of lateral thinking.

In this section I am looking at the specific creative sense of lateral thinking. This involves thinking tools like provocation and the use of the new word 'po'.

PATTERNS

As a self-organizing system the brain allows incoming information to organize itself into patterns. Those interested in exploring this matter further should read my books *The Mechanism of Mind* (1969) and *I Am Right – You Are Wrong* (1990).*

---

*Penguin Books, Harmondsworth, 1991

This pattern-making activity of the brain is most useful. Without the routine patterns that are established life would be impossible. A person who has been blind from birth is unable to see when sight is given to him or her, until the visual patterns we take for granted have been set up.

Reading, writing, talking, crossing the road, recognizing friends, recognizing food are possible only because of this superb pattern-making ability of the brain.

So we should all be immensely grateful for the pattern-making behaviour of our brains.

But patterns are not symmetric. In the diagram opposite there is a side pattern. As we go along the main track we are not even aware that the side track exists. But if we start on the side track, the route back to the first point is direct and obvious. In other words the route from A to B may be roundabout but from B to A is direct. That is what I mean by 'not symmetric'. This is a property of all patterning systems and there is nothing mysterious about it.

HUMOUR

Humour is an excellent model of lateral thinking. As we listen to a joke our thinking travels along the main track. Suddenly the punchline takes us across to the side track. Once there we can see the 'logic' of the connection. This process is shown in the diagram on p. 190. This sudden switch of perception is made more powerful if it draws upon emotions, prejudice and topical events. We accept the logic of humour just as we accept the unusual grammar of poetry.

One day far into the future brain transplants become possible. A manager is arranging a brain transplant for a key executive who has been injured in a car accident. He is offered a choice of several possible brains. One of them is five times as expensive as the others. He asks the reason for this high price. He is told: 'That is a very special brain – you see it has never been used.'

The logic is that an unused car is much more expensive than a used car. On the other hand an unused brain may not be much use. In the

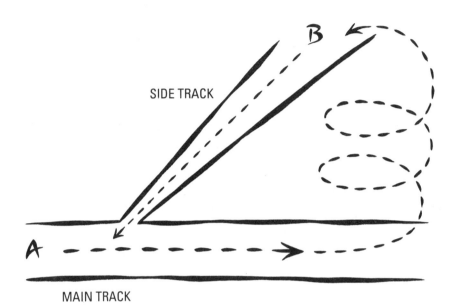

SIDE TRACK

A

MAIN TRACK

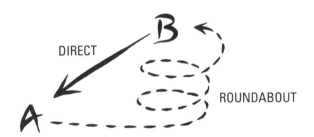

DIRECT

ROUNDABOUT

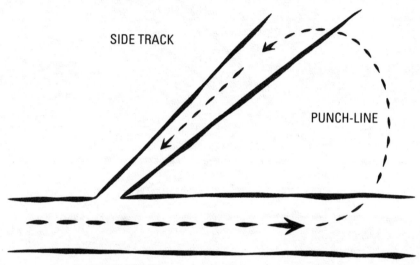

usual telling of this joke the unused brain is said to have belonged to a particular person, to a politician or to some ethnic group.

HINDSIGHT

In lateral thinking we develop deliberate techniques for getting us across to the side track. These techniques will be explained in the next few pages. Once we have got to the side track, then – as in humour – the path back to the starting point is obvious. That is why all valuable creative ideas are logical in hindsight. Because such ideas are logical in hindsight we have insisted that there is no real need for creative thinking, since better logic should be able to reach such ideas. This is simply not true in patterning systems. If it were true, only stupid people would have a sense of humour.

Provocation and Po

We come now to the specific techniques of lateral thinking. These techniques can be used deliberately by a thinker who needs to generate a new idea.

... 'Po cows can fly.'

... 'Po cars have square wheels.'

Both the above statements are totally unreasonable. They are contrary to experience and to the truth. Why should we make such absurd statements?

Provocation goes beyond hypothesis and speculation. In hypothesis and speculation we guess that something might be so but we cannot yet prove it. With provocation there is no pretence whatever that something might be true.

Because a provocation is not intended to be true we need some way of signalling to our listeners that a statement is put forward as a provocation – otherwise the listeners might think we have gone mad. We need a specific signal word for a provocation. Ordinary language does not contain such a word. The word 'suppose' and the phrase 'what if ...' are too weak, since they can be used to signal guesses that might be true. So several years ago I invented a new word, 'po'.

The word 'po' means: 'What follows is put forward directly as a provocation.' The letters 'p' and 'o' can be taken to represent 'p'rovocative 'o'peration.

Although it seems crazy and directly contrary to normal logic, a provocation is actually a 'logical' operation in a patterning system.

Because of the lack of symmetry in a patterning system we need some method for getting across from the main track of thinking to the side track. In humour the punch-line makes the connection. In lateral thinking we use the provocation. We use a provocation as a stepping stone, as shown in the diagram opposite.

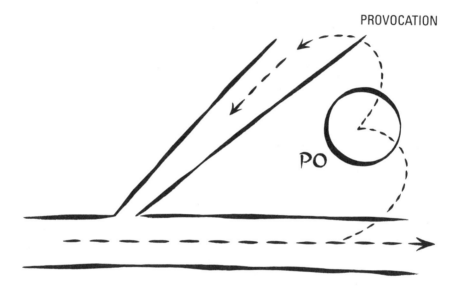

The first step is to set up the provocation. We then move from the main track to the provocation. This gets us out of the main track. We then move from the provocation to the side track. Once we are there, we might see in hindsight that we have a perfectly reasonable new idea. We forget about how we got there.

A lateral-thinking solution is never justified by how we get there (contrary to normal logic) but by the value once we have got there.

If we take a cross-section of the pattern diagram (see the diagram opposite) between points X and Y we get a picture that looks like two river valleys side by side. It is very difficult to escape from the main valley because we keep sliding back. In the same way it is difficult to escape from the main thinking track. We have to go against our natural thinking and experience, against the gradient, in order to escape. That is why provocation is necessary. Once we have got to the top of the 'ridge', we can find ourselves sliding down into the new valley.

It follows that a provocation should be provocative otherwise we might not escape from the main thinking track.

MOVEMENT

Once we have set up the provocation what can we do with it? We 'move' forward to a new idea. The operation of 'movement' is very different from judgement. I shall be explaining this operation of 'movement' in the next section. Provocation and movement always go together.

What could we get from the provocation 'Po cows can fly'? In our imagination we visualize cows flying around. What would happen? What would they be doing? Perhaps they would be roosting up in trees? It is at this point that we start to get an idea. A cow roosting in a tree could start to nibble the leaves. Perhaps we could feed cows on leaves from trees. Grass grows only in two dimensions, trees and leaves grow in three dimensions. Perhaps we could find quick-growing trees with leaves that are good for cows to eat (preferably directly, possibly after treatment). Leaves are full of protein. If space is limited we might get more 'leaf-grazing' per acre than grass-grazing. It may not work, but there is a new idea.

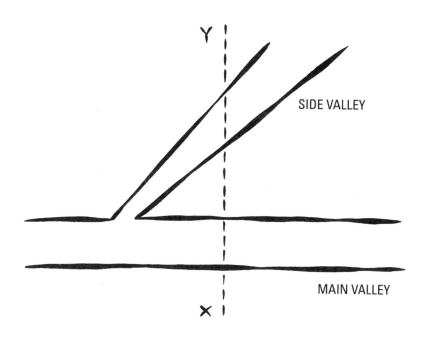

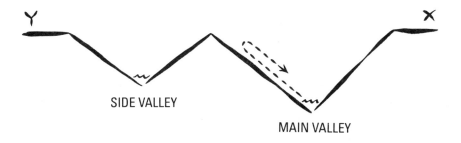

What could we get from the provocation 'Po cars have square wheels'? We imagine the car rolling forward. A wheel rises up on to its corner. We would get a very bumpy ride. But this rising is regular and we know exactly how high the car is going to rise. So if the suspension got 'shorter' this would compensate for the rise and we might get a smooth ride. This leads to the idea of a car designed to go over rough ground. For example a small wheel ahead signals back the bumpiness of the ground. The suspension then raises or lowers the axle to compensate for the bumps. The result is a smooth ride, as the car now 'flows' over the ground instead of 'bumping' over the ground. This is an idea I suggested as far back as 1975. Several car companies are now working on 'intelligent' suspension which does exactly this.

SETTING UP PROVOCATIONS

Where do provocations come from? How do you set up your own provocations?

RECEIVED PROVOCATIONS: You hear or read a stupid remark. This remark is not intended as a provocation. It may be intended as a serious idea or as a silly idea (for a laugh). You have a choice. You can dismiss the idea or you can choose to treat the idea as a provocation. Radar was invented this way. Some mad person suggested that a radio beam could be used to shoot down aeroplanes. From this crazy idea (because the power of such a beam was very low) came the useful idea of using the radio beam to 'detect' aeroplanes.

So you can choose to treat any received idea as a provocation.

REVERSAL: You look at the way things are normally done and then you deliberately go in the opposite direction. We normally try to make wheels as round as possible – so let us make them 'unround' or square. You normally pay to buy goods – so let us have the store 'paying' the purchaser. This might have led to ideas like trading stamps. What is the normal direction? What is the reverse (opposite) direction?

ESCAPE: In this method you look at some feature that we normally take for granted in the situation (it should never be a negative feature) and then we drop that feature or cancel it. For example we take for granted that watch dogs should bark. We drop that feature – escape from it – and so we get: 'Po watch dogs do not bark'. This leads on to the idea of small highly intelligent watch dogs that do not bark. Instead they quietly slink off into a corner where there is a button they have been trained to press. This button sets off a sophisticated alarm and security system – it could also trigger a tape-recorder playing a recording of many dogs barking.

WISHFUL THINKING: This should not just be a mild desire, like reducing the cost of an object by 10 per cent, but it should be a fantasy. You can say: 'Wouldn't it be nice if . . .' Wouldn't it be nice if polluting factories were downstream of themselves on the river? This leads to the practical idea of legislating that inputs from the river must always be downstream of the output – so the factory is the first to sample its own pollution.

OUTRAGEOUS: Quite simply this covers anything at all which you want to set up as a provocation. Po cars are made of spaghetti. Po breakfast cereals should grow in their packets. Po everyone votes every day on government decisions. This last provocation could lead to the idea that each day at 10 pm every householder would switch on an electric fire if that householder disagreed with an announced policy. The surge in electricity usage could instantly be measured at the power station – so giving an instant total vote. For a vote of agreement you switch on the fire at another time.

In general people are much too timid about setting up provocations. You are protected by the word 'po'. A provocation is meant to be a provocation. Whether you can use the provocation is not important. If you are setting up good provocations, at first you might only be able to use half of them. As you become more skilled at 'movement' you will be able to use more of them. A weak or timid provocation is very little use.

You should say: 'Here is my provocation.' Then you try to make use of it. It is a two-stage operation. Do not think of how you might use the provocation as you are setting it up.

SUMMARY

In any self-organizing system there is a mathematical and logical need for provocation in order to cut across patterns – and so get around the lack of symmetry. We use the new word 'po' to signal that a provocation is being offered. Five ways of obtaining a provocation are suggested: received provocations, reversal, escape, wishful thinking and outrageous. Do not be timid: a provocation should be provocative. Once you have the provocation you use 'movement' to move from the provocation to a new idea.

EXERCISES ON PROVOCATION AND PO

1. Which of the following statements are really provocations? In front of which statements should you put 'po'?
. . . aeroplanes should land upside down.
. . . hamburgers could be square.
. . . five hours is enough sleep.
. . . more women should be politicians.
. . . people should pay taxes according to their weight.

2. Set up an 'escape'-type provocation for each of the following items. You pick out some feature you take for granted and then cancel or drop this feature.
bicycle, library, elevator, birthday, house, tennis

3. Set up a 'reversal'-type provocation for each of the following items. You take the normal direction of action and then you reverse this direction.
collecting money for charity, choosing a career, friendship, watching television, cutting the grass.

4. Which of the following seem to you to be the most 'provocative' of the provocations? Place them in order with the most provocative first and the least provocative last.
. . . Po parents should ask their children permission before going out.
. . . Po each worker decides how long to work each day.
. . . Po the price of basic foods should be reduced.
. . . Po stupid people should pay less tax.
. . . Po cars should have no steering wheel.
. . . Po all cars should be coloured yellow.

5. Set up a 'wishful-thinking'-type provocation for each of the following. Use the phrase, 'Wouldn't it be nice if . . .'
school, parents, clothes, sleep, sports

6. Set up three different 'outrageous'-type provocations for the following items. The provocations must be outrageous.

telephones, human hair

Movement

A provocation is useless if we cannot do anything with it. We use 'movement' to move from the provocation to a new idea. Provocation and movement go together as a combined process.

The most important thing to keep in mind is that 'movement' is different from judgement. Many traditional approaches to creative thinking talk about 'delaying judgement' or 'suspending judgement' but this is much too weak. Just refusing to 'judge' does not indicate what the thinker should do instead. 'Movement' is an active operation that we can use deliberately. As we practise the operation of 'movement' we become more skilled at this operation. Eventually we can become so skilled that we are able to get 'movement' from almost any provocation.

The diagram opposite illustrates the difference between judgement and movement. With judgement (black-hat thinking) we compare what is before us with what we know. If what is before us is wrong, we reject it. With 'movement' we are operating outside the judgement/truth system. With movement we look at what is before us (usually a provocation) and we see how we can 'move' forward from this to a useful new idea.

In normal life the only places we use 'movement' are in poetry and metaphor. In both these cases we do not stop to say: 'Is this really correct?' Instead we move forward to see where the metaphor or image gets us.

Someone teaches you to play poker. You become good at poker. Then someone teaches you another card game, perhaps contract bridge. You also become good at that game. But when you are playing poker you use the rules of poker. When you are playing contract bridge you use the rules of bridge. You do not get the rules of the two games mixed up – you keep them separate. You are skilled at poker. You are skilled at contract bridge.

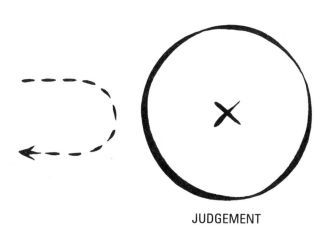

JUDGEMENT

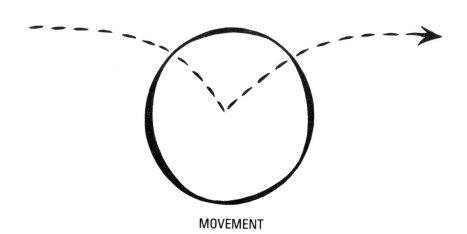

MOVEMENT

It is exactly the same with 'judgement' and with 'movement'. They are two separate games. When you are using judgement, you use skilled judgement (black hat). When you are using movement, you use skilled movement (under green hat). If you try to use something that is a mixture of both you will have a mess. When a carpenter is using the hammer he or she uses the hammer. When the carpenter is using the saw, he or she uses the saw.

WAYS OF GETTING MOVEMENT

There are a number of ways of moving forward from a provocation. Some of these ways are given here. These ways can be practised until skill in the operation of movement has been built up. Without such skill lateral thinking is not effective. It is not too difficult to set up provocations – the skill lies in getting movement from these provocations.

ATTITUDE: There is the general attitude of 'movement'. We make a general effort to go forward from the provocation. What does this lead to? What does this suggest? Where does this take me? What is of interest here?

MOMENT-TO-MOMENT: This may be the most powerful way of getting movement. We visualize the provocation in action – no matter how absurd this seems. So we visualize cows flying. We visualize a car bumping along on square wheels. We visualize a plane landing upside down. As we visualize these things we watch for what happens moment-to-moment. This is totally different from seeing what happens 'in the end'. In the end the car with square wheels would shake to pieces. In the end the plane landing upside down would crash. It is this moment-to-moment observation of the provocation in action that can lead to new ideas.

EXTRACT A PRINCIPLE: Could we pick out or extract some principle from this provocation and then make use of this principle in a practical idea? In looking for a new advertising medium we might say: 'Po we should bring back the town crier.' In the operation of the town crier we find an interesting principle: you cannot 'switch off' the town crier. We take this principle and look around for a medium we would be unable to switch off. We think of advertising telephones. If you did not want to pay for a call you press a special button and get a free call – but at intervals advertising messages come on the line and interrupt your conversation. In addition to extracting a principle we can also extract a key feature or a specific aspect of the provocation. This becomes a sort of 'seed' that we take to plant in order to grow a new idea.

FOCUS ON THE DIFFERENCE: How is this different from what we normally do? What are the points of difference? By focusing on these points of difference we seek to move on to a new idea. The difference between a plane landing upside down and the right way up is that in the upside-down position the wings would give downward thrust. This leads on to the idea of 'positive' landings. From this we can actually get to some useful ideas – such as cancelling a negative bias to get instant extra lift in an emergency.

Focusing on the difference is extremely important when a thinker is faced with that most powerful killer of new ideas, the phrase: 'This is the same as . . .' You suggest a new idea and this is dismissed by someone using that phrase. The phrase is so powerful because it does not attack the idea but simply indicates that it is not worthy of any attention since it is already known or being used. The only way to counter this phrase is to say: 'It may seem the same as (something) but let us focus on the difference . . .' You then proceed to list the points of difference.

SEARCH FOR VALUE: Is there any value at all in this provocation? Are there any directly positive aspects? Are there any special circumstances under which the provocation would have a direct value? The provocation 'Po ambitious employees should wear a yellow shirt or blouse' leads to several interesting ideas. For example, in a service business a customer would always try to choose a service assistant wearing a yellow shirt or blouse.

The more our minds become sensitive to value the more able we become to sense value in almost everything – including provocations. Once we have detected the value, we strengthen it, build upon it and try to make it practical. A dog detects a faint scent. The dog pursues that scent. The scent gets stronger. Finally the dog has tracked down its quarry. In the same way we can 'scent' value and can pursue that scent until we find value strong enough to be the basis of a new idea.

INTERESTING: What is 'interesting' about this provocation? The term 'interesting' covers many of the other ways of getting movement. There may be an interesting point of difference. There may be an interesting principle. 'Interesting' forms the third part of the PMI attention-directing tool that was described earlier in this book. A creative person notices and seeks out what is interesting. You may have to make the effort to find out something interesting.

SUMMARY

'Movement' is a deliberate, active operation that is distinct from judgement. We use movement to move forward from a provocation in order to find a new idea. Movement and provocation go together as a method of cutting across patterns and opening up new ideas. The ways of getting 'movement' include: attitude; moment-to-moment; extract a principle; focus on the difference; search for value; and 'interesting'. The first step is to set up the provocation. The second step is to use the provocation for its 'movement value'.

EXERCISES ON MOVEMENT

1. Use the 'moment-to-moment' method for getting movement from the following provocation:
Po each person decides how long he or she wants to work each day.

2. Use the 'extract a principle' method for getting movement from the following provocation:
Po all TV sets have a number in the corner of the screen which tells how many hours that set has been in use during that week (starts again at Sunday midnight).

3. Use the 'focus on the difference' method to get movement from the following provocation:
Po instead of tidying your own room, each person is responsible for tidying someone else's room.

4. Use the 'search for value' method for getting movement from the following provocation:
Po everyone celebrates two birthdays each year: your real birthday and an 'official birthday' on a date you choose.

5. You want some new ideas on restaurants. Set up a provocation

(using the escape method) and then get movement from this (using the 'interesting' method).

6. You are involved in a national campaign to encourage people to take more exercise. You need ideas for the advertising messages. Use the 'reversal' method to set up a provocation and then use the 'extract a principle' method to move to a new idea.

7. Use all the methods of movement, one after the other, to try to get the maximum movement from the following provocation.
Po at any time the age of the person driving the car must be shown on the back of that car.

The Random Word

The 'random-word' method is a powerful lateral-thinking technique that is very easy to use. It is by far the simplest of all creative techniques and is now widely used by people who need to create new ideas (for example, for new products). I first described this technique many years ago.

The history of inventions and ideas has many instances where a valuable creative idea seems to have been triggered by a chance happening (like the apple that is supposed to have fallen on to the head of Newton and inspired his concept of gravity as a force). How can chance events have a creative effect?

In the diagram opposite we see the usual non-symmetrical pattern. If we move forward from the starting point we cannot get access to the side track. We could use the provocation/movement method to cut across to the side track. If, however, we were to start at another point (shown in the diagram as 'RW'), we might connect up with the side track. Once there the path back to the point of origin is direct. A chance event can provide that point 'RW'. A chance event can allow us to enter the pattern at a different point. This gives us instant 'insight' or 'intuition' or the 'eureka effect'. It is said that Archimedes, playing around with the soap (or some other object) in his bath, suddenly hit on the idea of how to test whether a crown was made of real gold or not (by the difference between the weight of the crown in water and out of water).

Do we have to sit around and wait for chance events to spark a new idea? Do we have to sit under trees and wait for an apple to fall on our heads? We can do that. But we can also get up and shake the tree. We can produce our own chance events. That is exactly what we do in the random-word lateral-thinking technique.

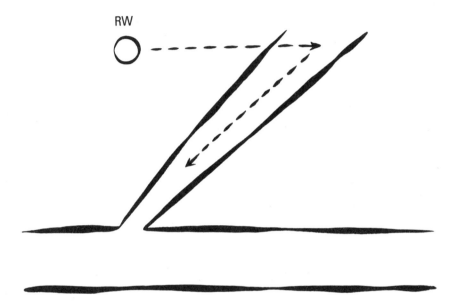

GETTING THE RANDOM WORD

We cannot choose the stimulus word because, if we chose the word, that word would merely fit in with our existing ideas (that would be the basis for the 'choice'). So instead of choosing the word we get a word by chance. That is why it is called a 'random word'.

You could have a bag full of thousands of words written on slips of paper. You put your hand into the bag and pull out one word.

You could think of a number of a page in a dictionary: say page 87. Then you think of the position of a word on that page: say the sixth word from the top. You open the dictionary at that page and count down to the sixth word. Here is your random word. If it is not a noun, keep going down until you come to the first noun.

You can close your eyes and circle your index finger above an open newspaper. You bring your finger down on to the newspaper and take the noun nearest to your finger.

You can have a list of sixty words (like the list given opposite). You glance at the seconds reading on your watch. If the reading shows 27 seconds you just take the 27th word from your list. If your watch can deal with 1/100ths of a second your list can have 100 words and then you stop the reading (on a stop watch) and use that number to get a word.

It is much easier to use nouns than verbs, adjectives or adverbs. If you construct a list of your own, they should be well-known words with many associations, functions or features.

Always try to use the first word you get. If you do not like the first word and try for another, and another, you are just waiting for a word to connect with ideas you already have. This is no use at all. So if the first word you get does not work move on to another technique and only try the random word again later.

LIST OF RANDOM WORDS

There is nothing special about the list of words given here. You can just as easily make up your own list.

horse	balloon	rocket
comb	telephone	mountain
snake	pencil	car
letter	tree	ladder
camera (5)	mouse (25)	glue (45)
elephant	television	cat
elevator	lawyer	radio
book	bee	table
cigarette	rain	heart
flag (10)	fire (30)	trap (50)
egg	bath	key
hammer	aeroplane	matchstick
sponge	guitar	copier
bell	paint	cactus
shop (15)	carpet (35)	prison (55)
tortoise	song	flower
spectacles	money	string
shoe	knife	eraser
nose	ice	gun
hamburger (20)	vote (40)	pin (60)

WHY IT WORKS

At first sight the technique seems absurd. How can a totally uncon-
nected word help generate ideas about a specific subject? If the
word is truly random, any word can help generate ideas about any
subject. This does seem a logical absurdity. Indeed, it would be an
absurdity in a passive information system. But in a self-organizing
information system the technique makes sense.

You set out from your house. You take the road you always take. If,
however, you were starting home from somewhere on the periphery
of the town, you would always increase your chances of arriving
home by a route which was different from your usual route. In other
words, as we move in from the outside, the patterns we use are
different from the ones we use if we move out from the centre. There
is no magic about it at all.

The brain is so very good at making connections that almost always any random word will stimulate ideas on the subject. Occasionally the connection between the random word and the subject is so direct that no new ideas are stimulated. Sometimes the random word simply leads us back to ideas we already have and it is difficult to keep away from these.

USE OF THE TECHNIQUE

We want some new ideas about copiers.
The seconds reading on the watch shows '19' so the word is 'nose' (from the list given here).
We say: 'Copier po nose.'
Nose suggests smell.
What value could smell have (movement)?
Perhaps a copier could give off different smells depending on what was wrong with it. So we could use smell as a fault indicator. If your copier is not working you just sniff. The smell will immediately tell you what is wrong.

You are asked to entertain some people and have to find something for them to do.
The watch reading is 49 seconds, so the word is 'heart'.
You might think of the little red 'heart' symbol that is now often used to mean: I "heart" New York' (I love New York).
So you set the group the task of suggesting other symbols that might suggest various things such as: I 'hate' New York; I 'don't know anything about' New York; I 'laugh at' New York; I 'am saddened' by New York.

So the technique is very simple to use.

We follow the associations and the functions of the stimulus word. We use the various methods of movement. We use aspects of the word as a metaphor.

Do not take too many steps in making the connection because if you take too many steps you will simply get back to ideas you already have and will not be using the special stimulating value of that random word.

Do not start out by putting down a list of aspects of the word because you will then just go down the list to find the aspect which fits ideas you already have. Instead, think of some one aspect of the random word and try hard to work with that aspect. Only after a good try should you go on to another aspect.

SUMMARY

Creative ideas are sometimes stimulated by chance events. The random-word technique of lateral thinking makes this process available as a deliberate thinking tool. A word that has been obtained randomly (without specific selection) is brought into contact with the focus area that needs the new ideas. Associations, functions and concepts suggested by the random word can lead to new ideas. The logic of the method is that, in a patterning system, if you start at the periphery the patterns you open up are different from those available to you at the centre.

EXERCISES ON THE RANDOM WORD

1. There are tables. There are chairs. There are beds. You want to design a new type of furniture that has never been used before. You will use the random-word technique. The random word is 'bee'. Furniture po bee.

2. You need to write a short story but you cannot think of a plot. What is the story going to be about? You use the random-word technique to get you started on an idea. The random word you must use is 'hammer'.

3. You are going away on holiday but you cannot find anyone to look after your dog for the week you are going to be away. You need some fresh ideas on this problem. You try the random-word technique. Try the random word 'camera'.

4. As manager of a store you want to find a way of encouraging your staff to be polite and helpful to the shoppers. You have run out of ideas so you try the random-word technique. Use the random word 'ice'.

5. You can never get near the telephone because your sister (or brother) is using it the whole time. What can you do about

this problem? Try using the random word 'key' to give you some ideas.

6. There is not enough space for cars to park in town. You break the problem down into three smaller problems. Choose one of these problems and try to generate some useful ideas using the random word 'cactus'.
Problem 1: discourage people from driving into town.
Problem 2: somehow provide more parking space.
Problem 3: reduce the need for people to drive into town.

7. How should parents control youngsters who never do what they are asked to do? Obtain a random word and use it to make suggestions on this matter.

8. Newspaper po balloon. Develop some new ideas.

Second Review Section

The first review section covered many specific thinking tools (PMI, OPV, six hats etc.). These were tools which could be used separately or together. A thinker who learned the use of these tools and became skilled at using even some of them would become a better thinker. Underlying all these tools was one powerful thinking 'operation'. This was the operation of 'attention directing'. This is the thinking operation that is key to the perception part of thinking. And the perception part of thinking is key to most day-to-day thinking.

This second review section covers far fewer tools. This second review section is concerned with some of the fundamental thinking operations. We need to know about and to understand these thinking operations. Some of these operations can be used as specific tools (like 'po' in lateral thinking), others can be the basis of thinking habits. Much of the time we carry out these operations without even considering them. The preceding sections have been an opportunity to consider these fundamental thinking operations.

TRUTH AND CREATIVITY

The big divide in the preceding sections has been between 'truth' and 'creativity'.

Truth maintains: 'This is the way things are.'

Creativity suggests: 'This is the way things could be.'

Both aspects of thinking are very important. Both aspects of thinking are needed.

At some point we have to start from reality. In the end we usually have to come back to reality. So truth is important.

Without creativity we would not progress or develop better ideas.

CRITICAL THINKING

Critical thinking is our check on truth: is this true?

There is 'game truth' when we have ourselves set up the game or system and we judge whether the game is being played according to our rules. Mathematics is an example.

Then there is 'reality truth' when we try to match what we are saying to the outside reality of the world around. There are different levels of truth. There is truth based on experience of ourselves or of others. There is checkable truth when anyone can check what we claim. Then there is truth based on some authority (science, reference books etc.).

We need to develop the thinking habit of always asking ourselves:

What is the truth value here?

What is important is the level of claimed truth. This can range from a claimed absolute certainty to something that is only offered as a possibility. Over-claiming needs to be challenged.

The next role of critical thinking is to check on the logic that is being used. With logic we seek to derive a further truth from truths which we already have.

We need to ask the habit question:

Does this follow?

A much more important question is:

Must this follow?

With a logical argument it is claimed that the conclusion must follow from the preceding step. We need to look closely at this 'must'. Very often it is claimed that something must follow because the thinker cannot imagine an alternative. If you can imagine an alternative, that destroys the 'must' aspect.

At the end critical thinking (black-hat thinking) may conclude:

This is false.

This is doubtful.

This is not proven.

This is proven.

CREATIVE THINKING

With creative thinking we are not so much concerned with proving something as with moving forward with possibilities. Once we have reached a new idea, we can set about proving its truth and value.

In logical thinking we seek to move step by logical step from where we are to a new position.

In creative thinking we can make jumps ahead and when we have reached a new position we then set about checking the value of that position.

Hypothesis, speculation and provocation are all ways of making that creative jump ahead. Sometimes we have to guess because we do not have enough information for action. In creative thinking we guess in order to have new ways of looking at information and in order to explore the possibility of new ideas.

The analysis of information is not sufficient to produce new ideas because the mind can see only what it is prepared to see – and that means the old ideas. We need to develop skill in speculation.

Speculation may range from a very reasonable guess (what we seek in a hypothesis) to a mere possibility to a provocation which makes no claim to truth whatever. The purpose of a provocation is to get us to look at something in a new way – not by presenting the new way but by jerking us out of the old way.

A creative jump ahead can pull our thinking forward. We lead from in front. Without creative thinking we lead from behind and we have to strive to push forward, building on what we know.

The creative attitude involves a willingness to go forward and to explore possibilities.

LATERAL THINKING

Lateral thinking is specifically concerned with changing ideas and perceptions. Attention-directing tools look after the 'breadth' aspect of perception. The lateral-thinking creative tools look after the 'change' aspect of perception.

Lateral thinking is based directly on a consideration of the pattern-making behaviour of a self-organizing information system (as in perception). Such systems allow incoming information to organize itself into routine patterns. Such patterns allow us to function in the world. We should be grateful for these routine patterns. But we cannot get across to the available side patterns because of the non-symmetry of patterns.

If we do get across to the side patterns we have humour or creativity. All valuable creative ideas must be logical in hindsight but this does not mean they are accessible to logic in the first place.

Two specific techniques are suggested for getting across to these side tracks.

The first technique uses a combination of provocation and movement. A provocation is an idea which does not exist in experience and has no truth value at all. We signal such provocation with the invented word 'po' to indicate that it is a provocation.

We then use 'movement' to move from the routine track to the provocation and then on to the side track (and a new idea). Movement is different from judgement. In judgement we compare an idea with what we know and reject the idea if it does not check out. With movement we operate outside the judgement system. We look at the idea to see how we can move forward from it.

There are specific methods for setting up provocations: received, reversal, escape, wishful thinking and outrageous.

There are specific methods for obtaining movement from a provocation: attitude, moment-to-moment, extract a principle, focus on the difference, search for values and interesting.

These lateral-thinking tools can be practised and then used deliberately whenever there is a need to generate new ideas.

BASIC OPERATIONS

The basic operations of thinking were reviewed. We need to be aware of these operations and it is useful to practise them from time to time. Any thinking performance uses a complex combination of these basic operations. Just practising the basic operations is not enough – just as exercising groups of muscles does not give us skill at a sport.

Using the carpenter model the basic operations were divided into three groups.

CUTTING: Focusing on part of a situation; extracting part of the situation; analysing the situation into its parts; expanding attention to include more than the presented situation.

STICKING: Making connections; recognition and identification; putting things together in synthesis; building things up in construction and in design.

SHAPING: This is a matter of comparing what is before us to some reference shape. So we have judgement, matching, hypothesis checking and comparison.

It is very important to remember that the philosophical description of thinking is not the same as the practical skill of thinking. A description of tennis is not the same as playing a game of tennis. Analysing thinking into its parts does not provide us with usable tools for thinking. Those tools have to be designed specifically for practical use.

FURTHER THINKING HABITS

Two other aspects of thinking were covered in the preceding sections.

Circumstances:

Some truths are universal, but many truths which are claimed as universal apply only under certain circumstances. This is a common cause of error in thinking and also of many disagreements (because one party is thinking of one set of circumstances and the other party of a different set of circumstances).

Often it is not a matter of arguing whether something is true or not true but of specifying the circumstances under which it is true. Often both sides in an argument can be right at the same time — under different specified circumstances.

So the thinking habit question is:

Under what circumstances does this apply?

Broad and Detail:

This aspect of thinking is part thinking habit and part operation. We need to get into the habit of carrying out the operation.

There are two habit questions:

What is the broad idea here?

How can this broad idea be carried out in detail?

The ability to move up and down from detail to broad idea and back again is a characteristic of the skilled thinker.

We extract the broad idea in order to change it or to find better ways of carrying it out. We extract the broad idea in order to simplify things and to understand them better.

When we are generating alternatives it is usually easier to lay out the broad ideas first. Then we look to see how these broad ideas could be put into practice as detailed ideas.

Working at the level of 'broad ideas' is similar to working at the level of 'concept' or 'function'.

SUMMARY

This part of the book has been concerned with fundamental thinking operations. Every thinker should have a clear understanding of these. In addition there are the specific creative techniques of lateral thinking.

REVIEW EXERCISES

1. 'It is the job of business executives to produce as much as possible. It is the job of government to look after the social values.' Is this true? Use your critical thinking.

2. 'There are only two ways of getting people to do what you want: reward or punishment.' Do you agree? Can you think of any other way? Use the random word 'mouse' to help you get ideas.

3. What is the 'broad idea' behind a shop window. How else might you carry out this broad idea? Give some detail ideas.

4. 'If you eat too much you lay down body fat. Women have more body fat than men. So women must eat more than men (relatively speaking).' Does this follow?

5. 'Children do not have enough experience of life to be able to make the right decisions. So children should listen to their parents.' Under what circumstances might this be true? What is the broad idea here? What alternatives might there be?

6. If dolphins in the sea can get all the food they need without too much effort, what do you think they should spend their time doing – if they are intelligent creatures? Give four broad ideas.

7. There are a lot of burglaries in an area. How would you reduce the number of burglaries? Use an 'outrageous' type of provocation to get some new ideas. Po . . .

8. Prisons only teach criminals to be better at crime. So there is no point in sending young criminals to prison. Is this a logical line of argument? Use the random word 'soap' to generate some alternative ways of treating young criminals.

9. 'If you do not like someone, you should not smile at that person.' Use your critical thinking on this.

Principles for Thinking

At this point we can put together some guiding principles for think-ing. This could have been done at the beginning of this book, but it would not have made sense. It will be seen that the principles arise directly from processes that have been covered in the book up to this section. So the principles become a sort of crystallization of what has been learned.

It would be possible to put down more principles or fewer principles. It would be possible to express them in different ways. There may be some you think I have left out. This is very much a matter of individual choice and what follows is my choice. It is difficult to keep the number of principles down to the twelve I give here. There are many other important principles that could have been included, but I believe that twelve is the maximum number that is practical.

1. Always be constructive.

Too many people get into negative habits of thinking. They enjoy proving someone else to be wrong. They feel that it is enough to be critical. There is a lack of the constructive and generative aspects of thinking. There are times when it is necessary to be critical. We need to esteem constructive thinking above critical thinking.

2. Think slowly and try to make things as simple as possible.

Except for a few emergency occasions there is no great merit in thinking quickly. A great amount of thinking can be done in a short time even if you think slowly. Always try to make things simple. There is no merit in complication (except to impress others). Is there a simpler way of looking at this?

3. Detach your ego from your thinking and be able to stand back to look at your thinking.

The biggest obstacle to skilled thinking is ego involvement: 'I must be right,' 'My idea must be best.' You need to be able to stand back and to look at what is going on in your thinking. Just as you might be objective about your tennis skills you should be able to be objective about your thinking. That is the way to develop any skill.

4. At this moment, what am I trying to do? What is the focus and purpose of my thinking?

Right now, what is the focus of my thinking? What am I trying to achieve? What tools or methods am I using? Without this sense of focus and purpose, thinking is just a matter of drifting along from moment to moment, from point to point. Effective thinking requires this sense of focus and purpose.

5. Be able to 'switch gears' in your thinking. Know when to use logic, when to use creativity, when to seek information.

In driving a car you select the appropriate gear. In playing golf you select the appropriate club. In cooking you select the appropriate pan. Creative thinking is different from logical thinking and from seeking information. A skilled thinker must be skilled at all the different types of thinking. It is not enough just to be creative or critical. You need to know when and how to use the different types of thinking.

6. What is the outcome of my thinking – why do I believe that it will work?

Unless you can spell out a clear outcome of your thinking you have wasted your time. If you have a conclusion, a decision, a solution or a design etc., you should be able to explain just why you think it will work. At this point how you got to the conclusion does not matter. Explain to yourself – as you would to someone else – why you think the outcome is going to work. If the outcome is a definition of a sticking point, a new problem or a better view of the matter, you need to say what you are going to do next.

7. Feelings and emotions are important parts of thinking but their place is after exploration and not before.

We are often told that feelings and emotions must be kept out of thinking. This may be true for mathematics and science, but where people are concerned feelings and emotions are an important part of thinking. But they need to be used at the right place. If feelings are used at the beginning, perception is limited and choice of action may be inappropriate. When exploration takes place first and when the alternatives have been examined, it is the role of feelings and emotions to make the final choice.

8. Always try to look for alternatives, for new perceptions and for new ideas.

At every moment a skilled thinker will be trying to find alternatives: explanations, interpretations, action possibilities, different approaches etc. When someone claims that there are 'only two alternatives', the skilled thinker immediately tries to find others. When an explanation is given as the only possible explanation, the skilled thinker tries to think of other explanations. It is the same with the search for new ideas and new perceptions. Is this the only way of looking at things?

9. Be able to move back and forth between broad-level thinking and detail-level thinking.

In order to carry out any idea we have to think in terms of actual details. So at the end we do have to be specific. But the ability also to think at the broad level (concept, function, abstract level) is a key characteristic of a skilled thinker. This is the way we generate alternatives. This is the way we move from one idea to another. This is the way we link up ideas. What is the broad idea here? How can we carry out that broad idea?

10. Is this a matter of 'may be' or a matter of 'must be'? Logic is only as good as the perception and information on which it is based.

This is a key principle because it deals with truth and logic. When something is claimed to be true the claim is that it 'must be' so. When it is claimed that a conclusion 'must follow' from what has gone before there is also an insistence on 'must be'. If we can challenge this and show that it is only a matter of 'may be', this may still have value but not the dogmatic value of truth and logic. Even when the logic is without error the conclusion only fits the perception and information on which the logic is based. So we need to look at this base. In games and in belief systems we set things up to be true so they are true within that context. In ordinary life we need always to distinguish between 'may be' and 'must be'. We need also to check what is claimed.

11. Differing views may all be soundly based on differing perceptions.

When there are opposing views we tend to feel that only one of these can be right. If you believe that you are right, you set out to show that differing views must be wrong. But differing views may be just as 'right'. A differing view may be soundly and logically based on a perception that is different from yours. This perception may include different information, different experience, different values and a different way of looking at the world. In settling arguments and disagreements we need to become aware of the differing perceptions on both sides. We need to lay these out alongside each other and to compare them.

12. All actions have consequences and an impact on values, people and the world around.

Not all thinking results in action. Even when thinking does result in action this action may be confined to a specific context such as mathematics, a scientific experiment, a game that is being played. In general, thinking that results in an action plan, a problem solution, a design, a choice or a decision is going to be followed by action. That action has future consequences. That action has an impact on the world around. This world includes values and other people. Action does not take place in a vacuum. The world is now a crowded place. Other people and the environment are always affected by decisions and initiatives.

SUMMARY

Twelve principles for thinking have been put forward here. For each principle there is an explanation which describes the scope and the importance of that principle. Some of the principles are concerned with how we operate the skill of thinking. Other principles are concerned with the practical use of that skill.

It is worth reviewing these principles from time to time.

EXERCISES ON PRINCIPLES FOR THINKING

The principles have been laid out without any direct references to the tools and other processes that are put forward in this book. This is so that these principles can also be of use to those who have not read this book.

The exercises for this section consist of taking the principles, one by one, and discussing them. This discussion must be constructive: Why is this principle important? Where is it most useful? Do people normally follow this principle?

In addition each principle can be related to the tools, operations and habits learned in this book. For example, principle 4 relates to 'Focus and Purpose' and AGO. Principle 7 relates to 'red-hat thinking'.

It will be found that most of the principles relate to one, or more, of the things that have been covered in previous pages. You can use the Contents list at the beginning of the book or the review sections in order to remind yourself of the material that has been covered so far.

PART FOUR

Structures and Situations

Up to this point in the book attitudes, habits, tools and operations have all been presented as separate items. It is true that with the six hats I did give suggestions for the use of the hats in a sequence. It is true that in the first review section I did give a sequence in which the attention-directing tools (AGO, CAF etc.) could be used. But both these suggestions were for additional use of the tools.

There is no single magic formula that will make a person into a skilled thinker at once. Many people put forward complex structures which seem very nice on paper but turn out to be impractical in use. You cannot go around with a complex formula in your head, and the formula is often too inconvenient to use.

All the tools and habits put forward so far can be used separately. If you take no more from this book than the PMI, that alone will improve your thinking. If you take the method of the six thinking hats, that will also improve your thinking. If you just take 'po' and the method of provocation, that alone will be very valuable.

A skilled thinker will hold several of the thinking habits in mind at the same time. For example, the thinker might have a strong sense of values (what are the values here?), a willingness to test the truth value (what is the truth value here?), and a consciousness of the need to work at broad-idea level (what is the broad idea here?). Another thinker might just have one habit in mind (under what circumstances is this true?).

It is not suggested that everything in this book will be learned instantly in one reading. You will have to go back again and again in order really to build up skill in all the things that are mentioned.

But my intention is that, even if the reader picks up no more than a few tools and a few habits, that will make a very worthwhile improvement in thinking skills. That is why the tools and habits have been presented separately. Think of the carpenter learning to use the hammer and the saw but not yet the plane and the chisel. With the saw the carpenter can cut things and with the hammer (and nails) the carpenter can stick things together. Not yet a highly skilled carpenter but much better than before.

At this point we come to structures and situations. A structure gives us a plan of what to do now and what to do next. Within the structures we use the tools and habits that have already been learned.

STRUCTURES

A cup is a structure. A staircase is a structure. An airport terminal is a structure. In all these cases the structure allows us to do things more easily. You could drink without a cup. You could climb up without a staircase. You might even get on to a plane by walking out on to the airfield.

The cup, the staircase and the airport terminal are structures that allow us to take one simple step at a time and so achieve what we want. You fill the cup, raise it to your mouth and drink. You take step after step up the staircase. The airport terminal arranges in sequence the steps of checking in, security, and walking to the right plane.

The thinking structures put forward in this book are organizing structures to help thinking. The structures lay out a series of steps. We take each step in turn. The steps help to direct our attention and help us to focus on one thing at a time.

Instead of having to plan our own structure on each occasion we just learn a structure and apply it.

There is no magic about these structures and they do not have to be used. They are presented as a matter of convenience. They help to reduce confusion in thinking. They also help with the discipline of thinking.

A structure can be a general-purpose structure which is suitable for most thinking situations or a special structure that is designed for a particular thinking situation.

SITUATIONS

There are many different thinking situations (exploring, organizing, planning, designing etc.) and I do not intend to cover them all in this book. I have selected three types of thinking situation because these three types are very important in ordinary life. These three types cover much of the thinking that we need to do. The three types of thinking situation that will be covered in the book are:

argument/disagreement

problems/tasks

decisions/choices

I intend to cover further situations in a later book.

I shall indicate the type of thinking required for the different thinking situations, the use of the tools and habits and also thinking structures for each situation.

SUMMARY

A structure is used to organize the steps of our thinking. There is a general-purpose structure and there are structures designed to help thinking in particular thinking situations.

TO/LOPOSO/GO

This is a very simple five-stage general-purpose thinking structure. This structure or framework can be applied to most thinking situations.

Each of the five steps in the structure is represented by a syllable. All five syllables have a consonant followed by 'O'. This is so the structure is easy to remember.

In addition there is a visual framework (diagram opposite) which puts the stages in order and also provides a visual reminder.

We can now look at each step in the structure.

TO:

Where are we going 'TO'?

'TO'wards what are we going?

What is the objective?

What is the destination?

What do we want to end up with?

What is the focus?

Problem definition and alternative problem definitions.

Use of the tool AGO to define objectives.

Use of the blue hat to define where we want to go.

The syllable 'TO' indicates the objective of our thinking. At this stage we need to define very clearly what we are trying to do. It is not enough to have only a vague and general idea of the purpose of the thinking. This must be precisely spelled out. This first step in the process should not be rushed. We should try to end this stage with a clear statement.

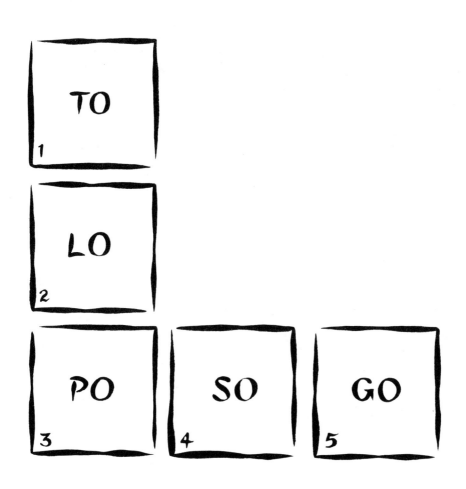

'The purpose of our thinking is to find a better way of handling garbage. We want to end up with a specific proposal and a plan to implement this proposal.'

'The purpose of our thinking is to come to an agreement regarding your contribution to the housework. We want to end up with an agreement as to what you are going to do to help.'

'The purpose of our thinking is to decide to which of these two people we should offer the job. We want to end up with a definite choice of one or the other.'

LO:

The word 'LO' comes from the old English word 'to look'. We sometimes might say 'lo and behold'. Some hymns use the expression. It means 'look at this'.

What have we here?

What is the scene?

What information do we have?

What information do we not have?

White-hat thinking.

Use of CAF. What are the factors to be considered?

Use of OPV. Who are the people involved here?

What is the context of the thinking? It may be friendly, antagonistic, legal, emergency etc.

What are the attitudes involved?

Who is doing the thinking?

What is the terrain?

The 'LO' stage is the stage of looking around. What is available? What are the pieces of the puzzle? This is exp'LO'ratory thinking. This is parallel thinking. We are scanning to see what we can see. We are not trying to reach conclusions.

At the end of this stage we want to have collected all the information we need – or specified what we would like to have. We want a good map of the scene. We want a list of factors that have to be considered. We want to know the context of the thinking. We want to know who is involved.

Think of an explorer who is given the task of mapping out a new country.

PO:

This is the 'PO' syllable that I invented to signal provocation in lateral thinking. Here the use is similar but broader. Here under 'PO' we put forward possible ideas as well as provocations.

What are the alternatives?

Use of the APC tool to generate alternatives.

Putting down some 'broad-idea' alternatives and then going on to work out the detailed way of carrying out these broad ideas.

Suggestions.

Proposals.

Possibilities.

Hypotheses.

Speculations.

Constructive ideas.

Green-hat thinking.

What comes up under 'PO' will depend somewhat on the nature of the thinking needs. If action is called for there will be action alternatives. If a problem has to be solved there will be solution alternatives. If an explanation is needed there will be alternative hypotheses.

This 'PO' stage is the stage of green-hat thinking, which means it is the generative stage. We put forward ideas and suggestions.

At this point we do not decide between the alternatives put forward. We just present them all in parallel.

'At this point we have four possible explanations of why the plane crashed.'

'At this point we have these three alternative solutions to the prob-lem of future water supplies.'

'At this point we have four alternative suggestions as to where we can hold the party.'

'At this point I have two alternative things that I would like for my birthday.'

All the alternatives should be put forward. There should be no pre-selection at this stage, but you may group the alternatives to indicate the most feasible.

SO:

This is the ordinary language word 'SO' which is used in one of its meanings.

'SO' what does this amount to?

'SO' what do we have here?

'SO' what do we do next?

This is the stage of choice between the possible alternatives.

We compare and examine the alternatives.

We need to come down to one choice of action (or explanation).

We do a FIP to assess the priorities.

We check the alternatives against the priorities and against the objectives of the thinking.

We assess each alternative using PMI, C&S and OPV.

What would happen if we used this alternative (C&S)?

What are the benefits and values (yellow-hat thinking)?

Does this fit what we know (black-hat thinking)?

What are the dangers and problems (black-hat thinking)?

We also seek to modify or improve ideas after black-hat thinking has pointed out the weaknesses.

The input to the 'SO' stage is a number of alternatives.

The output from this stage is a choice, decision or conclusion.

In cases where a single conclusion, decision or choice is not possible, the outcome has to be defined very carefully. What is the sticking point? Where have we got to? A new thinking task may be defined and the whole thinking process repeated on this newly defined task.

At the end of the 'SO' stage there must always be a clearly defined outcome.

'The conclusion is that we should stand firm and not give in to the demands.'

'I have finally decided that I want a camera for my birthday.'

'The decision is that we hold the party in John's barn.'

'The choice is that we offer the job to Mr Jones.'

'The outcome is that we cannot make a decision. This is because we do not have the costs of the alternative plans. We must now proceed to get those costs.'

'The outcome is that none of the suggested sites is suitable. We must now try to find some new sites.'

'The outcome is still disagreement. We have a clearer understanding of the positions on each side but no agreement. The sticking point is payment for weekend work.'

Anyone who is not happy with the definition of the outcome at the end of the 'SO' stage is entitled to put on a blue hat and to say that he or she is not satisfied and that a further attempt should be made to define the outcome.

In cases where action is needed (as with a doctor) it may not be possible to wait until there is more information. The best possible decision under the circumstances is the one that is used.

GO:

This is the normal use of the word 'GO' and it implies action.

Let's 'GO'.

'GO' forward into action.

Where do we 'GO' from here?

If there is no decision, choice or conclusion at the end of the 'SO' stage, then the 'GO' stage defines the action steps that must now be taken. This may involve collecting more information. Having a further thinking session. Setting a deadline.

What is the plan of action?

How do we implement this?

What practical steps do we take?

How do we put this into effect?

How do we monitor progress?

What is the fall-back position?

The output of the 'GO' stage is always action. There must always be a definite output from this 'GO' stage. Imagine you are walking. You take the next step. There must be a direction in which you take the next step. The output of the 'GO' stage is action for a purpose. 'Doing nothing' is only acceptable if this is actually a positive action. For example, not lowering prices because a competitor lowers prices. Or, not giving in to ransom demands. 'Doing nothing' as a result of indecision is not acceptable.

'Here is the action plan.'

'The output will be a report. The report will be written by Peter. The report should be ready by 12 October.'

'We will spend the next three months getting cost estimates from three contractors. Elizabeth will form her own team to select the contractors and to get estimates from them. We shall meet again to consider the matter on 3 May.'

'The decision is that the trip is cancelled. Please phone the others this afternoon to tell them this.'

'We have agreed that you should be home by 11 pm. Let us put that in writing so there is no more argument.'

'We have decided to allocate $6 million for the development of the new lawn-mower. John is going to put together a task force and a plan of action. We should get this by mid-June.'

'The first step is that we commission an opinion poll. Our next step will depend on what this shows.'

If at this stage someone is not happy that there is an actual 'action' outcome, that person can put on the blue hat to ask: 'What is the action outcome here?' The 'GO' stage must have an action outcome.

VISUAL STRUCTURE

The diagram on p. 238 shows the TO/LOPOSO/GO visual structure. I have chosen the 'L' shape because the vertical part of the 'L' indicates what we have before us (objective, information, possibilities) and the horizontal part of the 'L' shape indicates how we move forward (from possibilities to decision and then to action).

This separation of present input from action output is also suggested in the diagram on p. 239, where an input funnel leads into the 'PO' stage of possibilities. From the 'PO' stage an output funnel leads out to the world.

The two slashes in TO/LOPOSO/GO are there in order to make it more pronounceable and to suggest that there is an objective of the thinking and an action output of the thinking (TO and GO). In between the objective and the output, the thinking takes place. The slashes also separate the commonly used words 'TO' and 'GO' from the less commonly used words. Finally, the pronunciation of the syllable 'TO' is slightly different from all the other syllables (being pronounced as 'TO-O' not as 'TOE', which would have fitted 'LO-E', 'PO-E', 'SO-E' and 'GO-E'). This is a minor matter.

INTERACTION

The stages of this simple five-step structure are shown as separate and they should be kept separate otherwise they lose their organizing value. In practice, however, there can be interaction between the steps. For example, there is interaction between 'LO' and 'TO' because in collecting information you always need to refer back to the objectives of the thinking. This is what determines the relevance of the information. Similarly the generation of alternatives in 'PO' is based on what is available in 'LO'. Choice in the 'SO' stage may need to refer back to the objectives 'TO' and also to 'LO' (for example, in seeing who is involved).

SUMMARY

A five-step general-purpose thinking structure is given. This is made easy to remember by the names of the stages, TO / LO PO SO / GO,

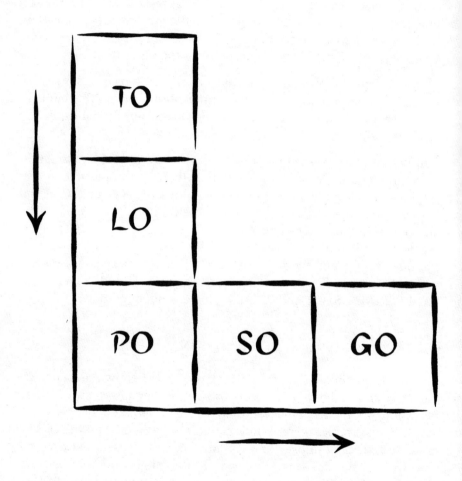

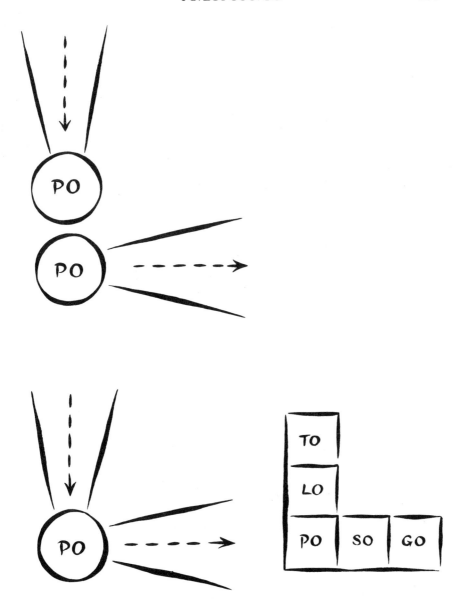

and by the visual 'L' diagram. The structure provides a series of steps that can be used for thinking about most things.

EXERCISES ON TO/LOPOSO/GO

1. Some visiting aliens have the ability to look and act exactly like humans, when they wish to. A pair of aliens have landed in a UFO and they are about to go shopping in a large shopping mall. Being trained thinkers they are using the TO/LOPOSO/GO structure. For each of the five stages put down what you believe the aliens might be thinking.

2. It is said that young people try drugs because their friends are trying drugs, because it is smart or fashionable, or because they are bored and want some excitement. Drug pushers who want money can be persuasive. It seems smart to try and nothing terrible seems to have happened to those who have tried. How could you persuade young people not to try drugs? Put down the steps of your thinking in the TO/LOPOSO/GO structure.

3. A young person aged eighteen years is given the opportunity to go to Japan for a year to work with a friend of the family who has just been posted to Tokyo. That person is trying to decide whether to go or not. Put down your thinking on the matter, using the TO/LOPOSO/GO framework. Try to come to a definite conclusion.

4. Most of the traffic into a town has to cross a bridge over the river. The bridge has been damaged by a barge and must be closed for major repairs. The person in charge of the operation uses the TO/LOPOSO/GO structure but a computer fault messes things up. Sort the items shown below into their proper boxes (TO, LO etc.).
. . . find diversion routes for the traffic.
. . . peak flow is 1,500 vehicles an hour.
. . . build a new permanent bridge near by.
. . . publish advance notices in newspapers and on TV.
. . . assemble a construction team.
. . . consider the business needs of the city.
. . . consider the voters in the city and suburbs.
. . . put up diversion signs.
. . . consider costs.
. . . half close the bridge to get people to find other routes.

Arguments and Disagreements

This is a very common thinking situation. Or, rather, it is a very common situation that needs more thinking than it usually gets. People have different views or opinions. People want to do different things. One person feels that another person should do a particular thing and the other person disagrees.

The range extends from quiet intellectual arguments to fierce emotional disagreements and disputes.

EMOTIONS AND FEELINGS

Emotions may be present right at the beginning. Indeed, the disagreement may arise because of those emotions. In such cases the substance of the disagreement is not that important, since the disagreement is only a way of showing the underlying emotions. It is important to be aware of this possibility because in such cases solving the immediate dispute may not be very helpful.

Emotions of anger, fear and especially resentment may be there from the beginning. In practice 'resentment' is a very common emotion or feeling. It is a mixture of dislike, jealousy, sense of unfairness, need for attention and similar ingredients.

I am not proposing in these pages to suggest solutions to disagreements that are a direct expression of long-standing underlying emotional dissatisfaction. Some of the thinking approaches may help in such cases, but counselling is likely to be more useful.

Then there are the emotions that arise in the course of the argument or disagreement. There is anger, fear, insults, shouting and bullying.

Use of the Red Hat:

The red hat can be used in two ways: as an exploration or as a label.

At the beginning of a disagreement or at any stage in the disagreement either party may suggest:

. . . 'Let's both put on our red hats and let's see what we find.'

Both sides explore their feelings and put them out into the open. You cannot be sure that the other person is being honest. You can express doubts and you can even say what you think the other person's red-hat thinking should have been.

The red hat is a way of exploring feelings and getting them out into the open.

When it is used as a label the red hat becomes a way of switching thinking. If the other party is being very emotional and very abusive you just say:

. . . 'That is good red-hat thinking.'

This does not imply that there is anything wrong with red-hat thinking but it does imply that red-hat thinking is not based on reason and is not a matter for discussion.

The red hat can also be used as a label to indicate your own feelings:

. . . 'Putting on my red hat, I feel angry about that suggestion.'

In this way you can make visible your emotional reaction to a suggestion. You do not have to give an explanation of your feelings.

Words:

There are many insulting words: 'stupid', 'ignorant', 'lazy', 'selfish' etc., etc. Most of these are adjectives.

These are really red-hat words: they express feelings but have no logical power. We try to point this out and so to remove such words from the disagreement.

. . . 'There you go again with another red-hat word.'

It needs to be remembered that many adjectives just express feelings and often the choice of adjective will show the feeling. For example if you call something 'smelly' it means you do not like that thing. But if you called the same thing 'scented' it would mean you did like it. Even in the most intelligent and apparently objective writing we can find this sort of thing. It is an interesting exercise to go through a newspaper and to circle the adjectives used. Most of these are 'feeling'-type adjectives which are used to make an argument. This sort of argument has no validity. It is rather like saying:

. . . 'My argument is right because this is what I feel.'

If someone says:

. . . 'Why do you wear that silly-looking dress?'

Then that person is simply saying:

. . . 'I don't like it when you wear a dress I don't like.'

The words 'right' and 'wrong' are used far too much in arguments. They add no value and create a great deal of trouble. They are far too absolute. We usually think that if we manage to prove the other party 'wrong' on some small matter, that other party is stupid and wrong in every matter. Obviously, the other party may be wrong in 95 per cent of what is claimed, and perfectly right in the remaining 5 per cent.

There are many words which seem to imply a lot and yet can be applied to anyone in any situation: 'uncaring', 'selfish', 'patronizing'. There is no defence against these words because they just mean:

. . . 'I want to think of you as selfish – you cannot stop me from thinking that.'

As a thinking habit you should watch the words used in any disagreement. The habit question to ask is:

Is this a red-hat word? Does it do anything except express feelings?

It is worth pointing out such words and trying to avoid them.

PERCEPTIONS

Perception, and not logic, is the basis of most disagreements and disputes. Each of the parties is being perfectly logical on the basis of his or her perceptions.

A mother wants her daughter home early because the mother's perception is of too much drink, bad company, drugs, sex and street violence. The daughter does not want to come home early because her perception is of well-behaved, good friends, normal parties, no drugs and also feeling stupid if you alone have to go home earlier than anyone else. Within their perceptions both are right.

An important source of differences in perception relates to the future. We can know the present but our extrapolations to the future depend on personal experience. A father wants his son to work hard to pass the tests. The father knows that if the boy does not get qualifications it will be difficult to get a good job. The son takes it for granted that he will have the same standard of living as his family and his friends. None of his friends seems to work hard, so working hard cannot be that important.

Most misunderstandings are based on different perceptions. You bump into someone who spills his drink. He thinks you are being aggressive. You know it was a genuine mistake.

You borrow something with the intention of putting it back. The other person thinks you have stolen it.

Perceptions have to be explored and defined.

The three basic steps in the settlement of disagreements can also be applied to perceptions:

1. These are my perceptions. This is how I see the situation.

2. This is how I think you see the situation.

3. How do you see the situation?

Steps two and three can be reversed. For example both parties may give their perceptions one after the other. Or, both parties may write down their perceptions simultaneously and then read them out. When the other party seems unwilling to define his or her perception, you do it for them:

... 'This is how I think you see the situation. If I am mistaken, tell me where I am mistaken.'

Once both sets of perception have been laid out 'alongside each other', it becomes possible to explore the difference. Perhaps both parties are right but looking at different things. Perhaps one party has better information on which to base perception. This comparison and exploration of perceptions can often be enough to solve the disagreement or at least to shift it to a constructive basis in which both parties work together to make progress.

... 'Why do I perceive things this way?'

... 'Why do you perceive things that way?'

VALUES

After differences in perception, differences in value form the basis of most disputes. Perception must come first because we need to perceive how values will be affected.

A government allows food prices to rise to market prices. The people object because they must now spend more and may not have the money. In the long-term perception of the government, the rise in prices will encourage farmers to produce more, so eventually there will be more food in the shops.

Sometimes the parties simply have different values. For young people the 'peer pressure' value is extremely strong. You want to fit in. You want to be one of the gang. You do not want to seem a freak. Parents find it very hard to appreciate the strength of this value. Parents think in terms of other values: health, danger, ability to earn a living, long-term security, what the neighbours may think.

Sometimes the parties have the same value but the proposed action affects the parties in an opposite way. A store raises its prices to make more profit. Customers have to pay more and resent having less money to spend elsewhere. Here the value of 'having more money' is the same for both.

The perception of risk is obviously a matter of perception. A girl wants to travel around India with some friends. Her parents perceive a risk from illness, robbery, violence etc. The girl, who has friends who have just returned from India without encountering any trouble, perceives the risk differently. That is a matter of perception.

But if both parents and daughter perceive the risk in exactly the same way, the willingness to accept that risk is a matter of differing values. The girl wants to be with her friends. The girl is interested in comparative religions. The girl wants adventure. The girl wants time to think before getting down to work. None of these values applies to the parents. They only see the dangers for their daughter and the possible expense and difficulty of having to rescue her.

The basic three-step approach applies to values as well:

1. These are my values (relevant to the situation).

2. This is how I see your values.

3.   What are your values?

As with perception, steps 2 and 3 can be interchanged. As with perception you can spell out the values for the other party if the other party is not willing to co-operate.

When the values have been laid out 'alongside each other', comparisons can be made. This is more difficult than with perceptions. With perception as soon as you see the possibility of a different perception you accept that possibility. With values you may see other values but are still left with the difficulty of deciding which values are the more important. Which values should decide the outcome?

Each thinker now makes a deliberate effort to show how the values of the other party can be looked after. The girl on her way to India can tell her parents that she will look after their fears by: having a good insurance policy; keeping in frequent contact; having a return ticket in her pocket; never travelling on her own etc.

Two friends rent an apartment. One values tidiness. The other values the freedom to leave things anywhere. Which value should prevail? There could be an agreement in which the person who values tidiness does all the tidying up but pays less rent. Or there could be an agreement that certain parts of the apartment must be kept tidy – but not all parts.

A general principle is that everyone has the right to pursue his or her own values (within limits) but not to impose those values on others. The person who wants to listen to loud music had better get some ear-phones or soundproof her room.

Creative effort and design are involved in trying to see how contradictory values can be made compatible.

Where it is impossible to satisfy both sets of values there can be an exchange of values.

... 'I will trade you this value for that.'

... 'You can have your friends in to a meal at any time – provided you do all the cleaning up.'

... 'You can borrow the car if you fill it up with gasoline.'

Bargaining, negotiation, compensation and extortion are all part of this exchange of values. There is a serious danger that in settling a dispute we may always insist on compensation for not getting our own way. This is a bad habit which makes the constructive settlement of disputes more difficult. You can set up false disputes, or refuse to see reason, in order to get some benefit. The parents may insist that the girl cannot go to India unless she first passes some examination.

We need to be on our guard against the introduction of irrelevant values:

Is this value related to the dispute?

A parent who has to stay up very late to collect a youngster from a party may suggest some compensation for loss of sleep. A parent who does not have to collect the youngster should not demand compensation just because he or she does not like the idea of the youngster getting home late.

LOGIC

On the whole logic plays a relatively small part in the origin of disputes or in the settlement of disputes (compared to perceptions and values). While perceptual insight can change values and emotions almost instantly, logical argument is usually powerless to do so.

Logic does have a role to play in the constructive attempts to satisfy conflicting values or to trade values.

In the case of normal arguments – as distinct from disagreements or disputes – logic is more directly involved.

Here the three habit questions encountered earlier in the book can be used:

1. What is the truth value here?

2. Must this follow?

3. Under what circumstances is this true?

The difference between the claimed truth value and the actual truth value is important. Something that is claimed to be absolutely true turns out to be based on hearsay of a friend. Information that is claimed to be true can be doubted:

. . . 'If that information is true then I accept your point.'

Where one point is said to follow from another point the listener is always on guard to see if the deductions 'must' follow.

. . . 'Your argument is that if there was no one else in the house it must have been my friend who took the book. You say that it could not have been a burglar because no burglar would just take one book. There is another possibility: that the book was not where you say it was. That you put the book down somewhere else and have forgotten where you put it.'

The ability to think of an alternative is usually the best way to show that something may follow but does not 'have' to follow.

The examination of circumstances is also very important in logical argument because – just as with perceptions – both sides may be right but under different circumstances.

. . . 'You are right. Everyone agrees that your dog is obedient and well behaved most of the time. But there are times when he seems to go berserk and become dangerous. That may be only one or two hours a year, perhaps when it is very hot, but with children around we cannot take that risk.'

. . . 'It is not a matter of whether man is good or bad. History shows that under certain circumstances man can behave very badly. Under other circumstances man can behave very well. Both points of view are correct.'

. . . 'Discipline is very important up to a point. Beyond that point discipline can stifle creativity and development.'

If arguments are undertaken on an exploratory basis it is usually possible to see why two people hold different views. When arguments are undertaken on a confrontational basis (as is usually the case) each side gets farther and farther from the other side and an outcome is rare.

Once again we can apply the three-step process:

1. This is the logic of my argument.

2. I believe this is the logic of your argument.

3. Tell me, once again, what is the logic of your argument.

With perceptions and values we may not know the thinking of the other party. With logic we should know because that is what we have been listening to. Nevertheless we can always ask for a simplification or summary of the argument.

As before, the opposing positions are laid 'alongside each other' and comparisons can be made. What is the basis for the difference? What matters are agreed upon? Can the two views be reconciled?

Quite often arguments are based on speculation about the future.

. . . 'If we raise the price of the shoes no one will buy them.'

. . . 'Everyone is going to have to increase prices soon. If we raise our price now we will not have to raise the price again when everyone else does. That way we lose some now but gain more later.'

We can put forward the bases for the speculations but sometimes we just have to accept that two opposing views are both reasonable. We then make our choice between them on another basis (for example the possibility of testing one of the ideas).

SPECIFIC STRUCTURE

The specific structure for the argument/disagreement type of situation is quite straightforward.

First of all there are four levels to be considered in turn:

1. Feelings

2. Perceptions

3. Values

4. Logical argument

At each of these four levels there are four things to be done:

1. Declaration and description for each party

2. Comparison: differences, similarities

3. Design

4. Trading: exchange and bargaining

Declaration:

The three basic questions:

1. These are my perceptions (feelings, values or logic).

2. This is what I believe to be your perception (feelings).

3. What are your perceptions (feelings, values, logic)?

In practice these questions are most important when applied to perceptions and values. The feelings and logical argument of each side are often apparent to the other side. What is less obvious are the perceptions and values underlying the feelings and logic.

Comparison:

The views of one side are 'laid alongside' the views of the other. There is no attempt to challenge them or to question the validity of the perceptions or values. The views can then be compared.

1. What are the points of similarity?

2. What are the points of difference?

There is an attempt to see how the differences arise. Is it a matter of information or looking at a different part of the picture?

Design:

At this point the attempt is to design an outcome that is satisfactory to both sides:

1. Can the differing views be reconciled?

2. Is there a new design that satisfies both sides?

Each party makes an attempt to show how the values of the other party can be looked after.

Trading:

This applies particularly to values. Some values can be given up in order to retain other values.

1. What values are most important to me?

2. What values can be given up?

3. What new values might be introduced?

Compensation can come into the picture at this point.

POWER DISPUTES

I have assumed in this section that both parties in the disagreement are interested in clearing up the disagreement. In real life this is not always the case.

In power disputes one side feels that it can win and does not want to compromise or settle the dispute. The best the other side can do is to make clear that winning is not possible and that even if it were possible it would be very costly and the result not worthwhile.

At other times there are people who have an interest in keeping the dispute going, perhaps because it gives them a sense of position and importance. If you can find out the values involved in keeping the dispute going, then you attempt to show how these values can be achieved in other ways and how keeping the dispute going might damage those values.

It is a pity that in power disputes each side seeks only to inflict the maximum amount of pain on the other side.

SUMMARY

The structure that can be used in argument/disagreement situations involves consideration of four levels: feelings, perceptions, values and logic. At each level there is an attempt to lay out 'alongside each other' the views of both parties. A comparison is then made of these views and an attempt to resolve the points of difference. The next step is to try to design an outcome that satisfies the values of both sides. If all else fails there is then a 'trading' of values in which values are exchanged until both sides feel satisfied.

EXERCISES ON ARGUMENTS AND DISAGREEMENTS

1. Two friends have agreed to go to a party together. But that evening one friend decides to stay at home to watch some new videos. The other friend is angry and they quarrel. Describe what might be the values for each of the friends.

2. A woman wants to start up a computer sales business on her own. She has a disagreement with her husband, who feels she should keep her well-paid job with IBM. Describe the possible perceptions on both sides.

3. There are plans to build a large tourist hotel right next to a small fishing village. The people of the village object because it will spoil their village and life style. The developer says that the hotel will provide more and better jobs in the area. Can the different values involved be fitted together?

4. On a trip to Egypt one person feels that you should never give money to beggars because it encourages them and also relieves the government of the duty to do something about helping them. Another person feels that if you are fortunate enough to have money you should share a little of it with those who are less fortunate. What is the perceptual basis for this disagreement? Can the different perceptions be brought together?

5. 'It is better to get a professional lawyer otherwise you lose out in a dispute.'
'Once it is in the hands of a lawyer the dispute can only grow and there is no chance of a settlement – because lawyers have to earn a living.'
Can these two logical arguments be fitted together?

6. A stray cat comes to a house where a well-fed cat is in residence. Write a dialogue in which the stray cat uses 'value exchange' to persuade the resident cat to allow her to stay.

7. You borrow the family car and are involved in a crash. Describe the values, perceptions and logic on both sides when you get home.

Problems and Tasks

You need to get to the airport in a hurry but your car will not start.

You meet someone you like and you would like to get in touch with that person again – but you do not know how.

The smell from the local garbage heap is getting worse.

You are travelling in a foreign country and you are thirsty but you do not know if the water is safe to drink.

There is too much stealing from the store you manage.

You are not able to recruit the staff you need.

Your competitor comes out with a better product and your sales slump.

The infection is getting worse but the patient is allergic to the antibiotic she really needs.

Your friend is very upset because he has misunderstood something you told him.

There are problems all around, some major, some minor. A problem is an interruption, an obstacle or a block to the smooth running of what we are doing. Sometimes we can draw back or give up but mostly we have to try to solve the problem.

On the whole we do not have to go looking for problems. Problems make themselves visible. You can try to ignore a problem (like the smell from the garbage dump or a neighbour's gossip) but mainly you have to try to solve problems.

... 'I want to do this, but I cannot because there is this problem.'

TASKS

Problems are provided by the world around. You do not have to go looking for them. The motivation for solving problems is high because we have to try to solve problems.

Tasks are problems that we set ourselves.

We need to solve problems.

We want to 'solve' (carry out) tasks.

With a task we set up a problem for ourselves. We decide that we want to do something and then we have to look around to see how it can be done.

An inventor sets herself the task of designing a tyre that cannot be punctured.

A gardener sets himself the task of growing a rare type of hyacinth.

A researcher sets himself the task of finding a vaccine for a dangerous virus.

A girl sets herself the task of finding homes for four kittens.

A politician sets herself the task of getting elected.

A boy sets himself the task of giving a party that will be remembered.

A detective sets himself the task of finding out who did the murder.

A historian sets herself the task of learning Russian so that she can read original documents.

In some of these examples (researcher, kittens, detective, historian) there is an overlap between problem and task, since the tasks may seem to fall within the person's normal activities. The question is: do you have to do this or do you want to do this?

We set out to solve problems and tasks in exactly the same way. So it is not important to distinguish between the two from the point of view of solution. What is important is that we should, from time to time, be willing to set up tasks for ourselves.

Ambitious people are always setting tasks for themselves. Then they move ahead to carry out those tasks. Lazy people do not set tasks but simply go along from day to day and solve the problems that arise.

Even people who do set tasks are usually too timid in the tasks they set. Now and again it is worth setting tasks that at first seem impossible. Then you start working on the task and you find it gradually becomes possible.

GUESSING AND ESTIMATING

How do we get to where we want to go, from here?

There is the starting point, there is the known destination, and here is the unknown route.

The first step is to guess or estimate in which direction we would have to travel. This guess might be very broad.

... 'It seems to me that we should head north.'

That is a start. Next we look around for some roads that are going north. We may find some. We examine the potential routes. When we have some clear alternatives, we choose between the alternatives.

Good mathematicians are always able to estimate the answer in broad terms before proceeding with detailed calculations. This broad estimate provides a guideline and prevents mistakes.

With problems and tasks we use a broad idea (guess or estimate) in order to give us a sense of direction. Once we have the broad idea or several broad ideas, we can see how the broad ideas can be carried out in detail. We may find this is quite easy or difficult. As I indicated in the section on broad ideas and detail, the broad idea is a way of generating alternatives.

THE PROBLINK™ METHOD

This is a problem-(and task-)solving method that is helped by a visual structure.

There is the starting position.

There is the route.

There is the destination.

The diagram opposite shows the general starting position, the general route and the general destination.

The destination is the objective of our thinking (AGO), the place we want to reach. The first step is to 'drop' ideas down from this destination box. These can be either situations that provide a solution to the problem or sub-objectives that once reached will enable us to move forward to a solution.

As an example let us take the problem of the neighbour who parks his or her car in front of our garage. The obstructing car could also belong to guests visiting the neighbours.

The ideas that we 'drop' down from the objectives box might include:

... the offending cars are parked elsewhere

... obstructing cars can be moved

... no cars are parked in front of the garage

... the neighbour knows not to park there

Any of these situations would be helpful to us in solving the problem.

For the next step we move back to the 'route' part of the second diagram and we proceed to 'drop' broad ideas from the route. These ideas might be very broad or may be almost detailed. They are ways of getting to the destination. For the car-parking problem the broad ideas might include:

... make it impossible to park there

... warn the neighbour

... put up a notice

... talk to the neighbour

... complain to the neighbour

This list is not comprehensive. The list may also include ideas that overlap (put up a notice, warn the neighbour) but this does not matter. Just put down the ideas. They can be sorted out later.

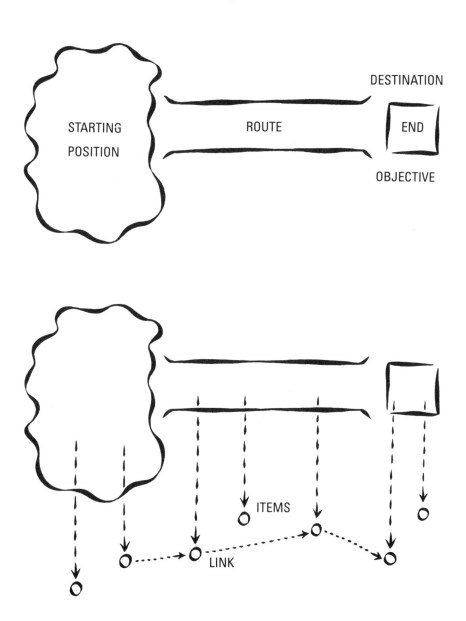

The final step is to move back to the starting situation. Here we do exactly the same thing. We 'drop' down features or elements. This need not be a complete analysis of the situation – though it could be. For the car-parking problem we might 'drop' down the following features.

. . . the neighbours

. . . the neighbours' guests

. . . they might know but forget

. . . they might think it does not matter

. . . they might think the garage owners are away

. . . they might know but not care at all

What we have done here is to pick out or rather 'drop down' aspects, features, elements of the starting position. There is no need to be comprehensive at first. We can go back and do that later. The purpose of the diagram is to stimulate ideas.

'Link':

At the end of the first stage we have a diagram that looks like a small rainstorm.

Our task is now to find a way from the starting position to the end position by linking up some of these items.

We can start at any point and move in any direction (towards other items).

We could start with the destination item, 'cars parked at that spot should be movable'. This can be linked up with the 'notice' item under 'route'. This suggests that we put up a large notice saying that cars left at that place must have the ignition key in place to allow for moving if the garage is needed. This seems a reasonable request. But most people would not like to risk leaving the key in the car, because of theft, so they would choose to park elsewhere. The idea of the car 'being movable' might link up with the ideas of 'warning'. A notice might then warn that cars parked there could be towed away.

The destination item 'parked elsewhere' might also link up with 'notice'. A notice on the garage door might give details of alternative nearby parking (a constructive move).

We could now try to make some links from items under 'route'. If we made parking 'impossible', this would link up with the starting item of neighbours who knew about the difficulty but 'did not care'. It would also link up with the destination item of 'no cars parked there'. At this point we are making general links so we do not see how the broad idea of 'impossible' can be carried out.

We may take the route item 'talk' and link this up with 'neighbours'. We might just talk to the neighbours or talk to them again and again until it became a real nuisance for them.

We could also try and make links from the 'starting-point' items. For example we could take 'forgetting' and see what this might link up to. It could link up with 'notice' or with 'impossible'. The item of 'guests' would also link up with 'notice' or 'warning'.

Route:

Once some links have been formed we see if we can extend these links so that we have a complete route, through the items, from the starting position to the end position. For example the link might be: guests–notice–park elsewhere. It might be: 'don't care'–impossible–not parked there. We make as many such links as possible.

Detail:

The routes we now have are mostly at the level of 'broad idea'. For example the broad idea of making it 'impossible' to park in front of the garage is a very broad idea. We now need to see how that idea can be carried out in practical detail. We can indicate this on the diagram by putting a triangle under the broad idea (see diagram overleaf). This is an indication that the broad idea must be worked out in detail. So we look around (APC tool) for alternative ways of making parking impossible. This focus could itself become the start of a new thinking session.

... we could put posts which could only be laid flat if you had the key.

... we could put slabs which would allow you to drive into the garage but not park sideways across the entrance.

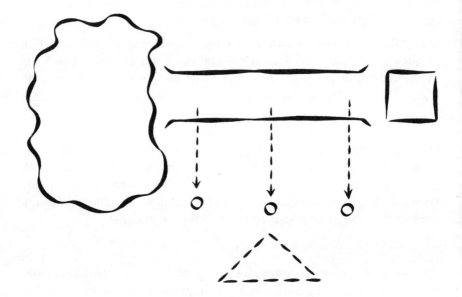

... we could have an old car of our own which we always kept parked in that place.

For any route that passed through the point 'notice' we would need to say in detail what would be on the notice:

... leave keys in ignition.

... this is where you can park (giving alternatives).

... your car may be towed away.

At the end of the detail stage all broad ideas that are part of a 'route' must be spelled out in detail.

We then put together our alternative 'routes' or solutions to the problems. These are the routes by which we can get from where we are to where we want to be.

SELECTION OF ALTERNATIVES

The alternative solutions to the problem (or task) may have been obtained through use of the Problink® method or they may have come from any other source. For example you may have used a simple TO/LOPOSO/GO approach.

The selection of alternatives now becomes a matter of 'choice and decision'. This type of thinking situation will be covered in more detail in the next section. Nevertheless, we can consider here the general method of selecting an alternative.

Objective:

Do all these alternatives satisfy the objective (AGO)? If an alternative does not satisfy the objective, it is dropped or modified in order to satisfy the objective.

Feasibility:

Is the alternative feasible? Can it be done? Is it legal? This will require black-hat thinking. Putting posts in the road may not be legal.

Priorities:

These will have been decided in advance (FIP). One priority might be to be on good terms with the neighbours. Another priority might be cost. Which alternatives best meet the priorities? Simplicity is usually a basic priority. Which alternative is simplest to try (even if it is not the best alternative it is worth trying first if it is the simplest)?

Values:

What are the values involved? What are the values for the different parties concerned? If the neighbour has nowhere else to park this is different from if the neighbour parks there out of carelessness. If there is nowhere else to park, then the neighbour could give you a permanent set of car keys so that you could move the car whenever you needed to. This way the neighbour's value of a parking space and your value of access are both looked after.

General Assessment:

This would include yellow-hat thinking. It would also include looking at the consequences (C&S). An OPV would be done if it had not already been done in order to see the thinking of the other people involved – for example the neighbours might be upset to find a fierce warning when a quiet word would have been enough. Finally a PMI could be used on each alternative.

ACTION

At this point an alternative should have been chosen. It may be a matter of trying out the simplest alternative and then moving on to another if the simple one does not work. Practicality is always important. Where other people are involved their thinking, feelings and values are also very important. It is rarely a matter of the perfect solution in isolation. Real-life thinking is never in 'isolation'.

Action steps are laid out and then implemented. This is the 'GO' part of TO/LOPOSO/GO.

NEW PROBLEMS OR TASKS

At any point in the thinking it may be necessary to define a new problem, task or sticking point which then becomes the focus for a specific thinking session in its own right.

In a similar way a major problem may be broken down, from the start, into sub-problems. Each of these sub-problems is then given direct thinking attention.

One of the most important parts of the skill of thinking is the ability to re-define focus areas and to define new problems.

. . . 'Right here it seems to me that we have a different problem. The problem is: how do we get on friendly terms with the neighbour?'

. . . 'We could define that as a new problem.'

. . . 'In the course of this morning's thinking we have defined four focus areas or problems that need thinking about.'

Problem-finding is the same as task-setting. For example, in improvement if we are happy with the way things are then nothing gets improved unless there is an actual problem. With task-setting we can focus on something and give ourselves the task of finding a better way to do it.

SUMMARY

Problems make themselves known. There is an obstacle to what we want to do. We do not deliberately create our own problems. With task-setting we do set up problems for ourselves. We define where we want to go and then try to find the way there. Most people are too timid about task-setting.

The general structure for problem-solving is the generation of alternatives and then the selection of an alternative.

The Problink™ method is a visual structure that allows us to make links at the broad-idea level and then to see how these may be carried out in detail. The selection of the best alternative depends on fit with objective and priorities, a consideration of feasibility and the values involved. In real life there are no solutions in isolation. There is a world around with people in it.

EXERCISES ON PROBLEMS AND TASKS

1. Put down three major and three minor problems that you have.

2. A girl moves with her family to a new district. Put down four tasks that she might set herself.

3. A manager cannot find the right staff. Set out a Problink™ diagram and drop items for each part.

4. There is a lot of theft from a food store by shoppers. A Problink™ diagram gives the following items for each part. What links can you make?
Starting position: food displays, thieves have no fear, shoppers not interested, cannot watch everyone.
Route: warnings, TV cameras watching, detectives, rewards, occasional publicized arrests.
Objective: decreased theft, more fear, shoppers more helpful.

5. In the task of designing a new playground for children the following 'broad ideas' are put forward. Can you find detailed ways of carrying them out?
'something new every day', 'children build their own things',
'parents and children can play together'.

6. The cat has four kittens. They are going to be killed. A girl (or boy) sets out to find homes for the kittens. Do a full task-solving exercise, using the Problink™ diagram and ending up with an action plan.

7. The smell from the local garbage dump is increasing. Which of the following solutions might be best?
... complain.
... organize the neighbourhood to complain.
... change houses, move to another area.
... use more scent in your house.

8. Your friend is upset because he has misunderstood what you have told him. Is it a good solution to be upset with him because he misunderstood you?

Decisions and Choices

We can look at three possibilities in practical thinking:

1. I have no idea at all about what to do.

2. There is only one course of action.

3. There are several possible alternatives – which do I choose?

If you have no idea at all about what to do, you may need more information. Perhaps there is a way of doing what you want to do and if you find out about this way you can use it. You may need to use the problem-solving techniques. You may need to use creative thinking (and lateral thinking) in order to generate some new ideas.

If there is only one course of action, you may have to follow that course of action. But before doing so it is useful to see if there might be other possible courses of action. Sometimes you think there is only one course of action because that is all you can find. So this situation becomes the same as the first situation: how can I find another course of action? If you do succeed in finding other courses of action, you now have alternatives and the situation becomes the third one: how do I choose between alternatives?

Sooner or later most thinking situations in real life end up with a number of alternative courses of action. You have to make a decision. You have to choose between the alternatives. That is why this is the last major item to be covered in this book.

Apart from having to choose between alternatives in problem-solving, planning, designing etc. there are also situations which directly demand choices and decisions.

Do I want to go to this party?

Should I marry him?

Shall I buy that?

Where shall we go on holiday?

Do I take this job?

What career shall I choose?

Is it time to buy a new car?

Do I dismiss my assistant?

Who do I vote for?

What treatment shall I choose?

Do you want this surgical operation?

EMOTIONS

In the end all decisions and choices are emotional. On the whole we do not feel this is a very good way to make decisions or choices, so we sometimes try to apply some thinking.

The purpose of thinking is to so arrange matters that when we do finally make the 'emotional choice' it is on a much better basis.

If you go into a shop and buy the first shoes you find that may not be very sensible. If you could have all the shoes available in your town, put out on a table in front of you with all the prices and necessary information, you would feel that your choice was likely to be better. The purpose of thinking is to try to arrange the choices in this way.

You may feel that final choices should not be emotional but should be logical. This may be the case in technical areas, but where people are involved the final choice is emotional. Suppose you say: 'I am going to make the most practical choice in this matter.' What does this mean? It means that your choice is based on 'fear': fear of making a mistake, fear of risk, fear of losing money, fear of a lot of trouble, fear of what others say, fear of seeming silly, fear of being impractical.

In the end most choices and decisions are based on three emotions: greed, fear and laziness.

GREED: More money, achievement, being ahead, being noticed, acquiring more skill, getting new friends, being better at your hobby, better self-image etc. I am not using 'greed' in a bad sense but in the sense of achievement and of wanting more.

FEAR: Fear of making a mistake, fear of being silly, fear of upsetting others, fear of the unknown, fear of losing money, insecurity of any sort, fear of change. Fear may prevent us making one type of decision and fear may force us to make another type of decision.

LAZINESS: In a sense this is the opposite of greed but it also has elements of fear. Not being motivated, not wanting to make an effort, being content, not wanting the bother and hassle of doing something, not wanting to be caught up in complicated matters, not wanting problems, wanting an easy life.

When you have made a decision it is a useful simple check to say to yourself: 'What contribution have greed, fear and laziness made to this decision?'

MINOR DECISIONS AND CHOICES

There is a difference between choosing which dress to wear to a party and choosing a future career. There is a difference between deciding to go to a conference and deciding to invest millions in a new project.

Simplified structures are needed for minor decisions and choices.

The Six-Hats Structures:

1. What do I want to do? (red hat)

2. Why not? (black hat)

3. Can the difficulties be overcome? (green hat)

4. Do I still want to do it? (red hat)

This structure is simple to apply if you do want to do something. But what about those cases where you do not want to do something but feel that you should?

In such cases you bring in the yellow hat immediately after the red hat.

1. I do not want to do this (red hat)

2. But there are benefits (yellow hat)

3. What are the problems? (black hat)

4. Can these be overcome? (green hat)

5. What do I feel now? (red hat)

It is obvious that if our initial emotional reaction to something seems adequate, we do not feel we have a decision or choice situation. If someone offers to sell you a broken watch, your decision is automatic. So we feel we have a need for thinking when we have doubts about our first reaction. Therefore we use the six hats to explore away from that first reaction. So if the feeling is positive we use the black hat to follow. If the feeling is negative we use the yellow hat to follow.

Attention-directing Tools:

The simplest assessment of all is to use the PMI. On each of the alternatives you simply do a PMI. You list the Plus points, the Minus points and the Interesting points. Then you see what you feel. Do not count the points. One minus point may be more important than ten plus points. Just see what you feel.

Another assessment tool is the C&S. You take each possible choice and imagine you have made that choice. Then you follow the consequences of that choice into the future: immediate, short-term, medium-term and long-term. When the different roads have been laid out, look at them. See which road you fancy.

For a fuller assessment we could use the attention-directing tools in the following sequence:

1. AGO: which alternative fits best with what I really want?

2. FIP: how do the alternatives fit the priorities?

3. OPV: what about values and other people?

4. C&S: what would follow, what consequences?

5. PMI: a final, general, assessment.

We explore our perceptions in this way until we get a feeling about the choice we want to make.

MAJOR DECISIONS AND CHOICES

Here we have to assume that you are going to have all the thinking time you need. There is no virtue in hurry. You can therefore go through a much more detailed assessment.

A check-list can be applied to each alternative.

Objective and Priorities:

Does this alternative reach the objective? If an alternative clearly does not meet the objective it is dropped. Sometimes the objective may have to be changed. If you are choosing where to buy a summer house and come up with the alternative of buying a boat, the objective is not to choose a summer house but a summer place.

In practice it is quite difficult to see if alternatives meet the priorities. One alternative may exactly fit a priority. Another alternative may only just fit. You may end up with an 'A' list of alternatives that clearly meet all the priorities and a 'B' list of those that meet only some. If an alternative does very badly at meeting priorities it can be dropped.

Benefits:

This is yellow-hat thinking. What are the benefits to the decider/chooser from each alternative? Why is this a good choice? Why should I want to do this? If I had to describe the benefits to myself, how would I list them? At this point I am not referring to the values affecting other people but the direct benefit to the doer.

If there are no profits in a business venture and no other benefits, why do it?

This is a very important step. If the benefits are absent or poor, the alternative can be dropped instantly.

You may still like an alternative that does not fit all the priorities – but it is difficult to see how you could like an alternative which offered no benefits.

Feasibility:

Can this be done? Can this be carried out? Is it possible? Is it legal? Is it practical? Is it mechanically sound?

You could argue that the 'feasibility test' should have come first because if an alternative is not feasible why bother to assess benefits? This may be true in science, in engineering and in mathematics but it is not true in real life.

In real life feasibility is often a matter of degree. If you really like an expensive house you might be willing to borrow money to buy it. If you really like something, there may be a way of making it feasible. That is why I put benefits before feasibility. If the benefits are great, we make an effort over feasibility – we may not succeed.

Difficulties and Dangers:

The black hat is directly concerned with the judgement of feasibility. The black hat is also concerned with examining difficulties and dangers. What are the problems? What are the friction points? What are the dangers?

These are more the difficulties involved in taking that course of action (for example high cost) rather than the difficulties in the future – since these will be covered later. Something may be feasible but still have difficulties, obstacles and delays (like obtaining building permission). Contingencies should be considered here: 'This is worth doing if . . .' The black hat points out these 'ifs'.

Impact:

If you set out to build a factory in parts of the USA you have to have an 'environmental impact' study done to show the effect of your decision on the environment.

In the same way we need to examine the 'impact' of each alternative on other people (close and not so close), on values, on other projects, on life style, and on the environment.

What are the effects of this course of action? What are the ripples? We may not know the exact answers and may be able to talk only in possibilities and probabilities. But we do have to look at the impact.

Consequences:

It is obvious that benefits, difficulties and impact all include elements of consequences since the effects will happen in the future after the decision is made. It is still useful, however, to have a specific point on the check-list where we look directly at consequences. Even if part of this overlaps with what has gone before. Overlap is not a problem – leaving things out is a problem.

We look at the immediate consequences of making the choice: paperwork, legal matters, informing people etc. We look at the immediate consequences not only of the choice but also of our making the choice. Then the short-term consequences followed by medium-term and long-term. The actual time-spans may vary according to the decision. The time-span for choosing to buy a car is different from that for choosing a career. In general short-term is up to one year. Medium-term is up to five or ten years. Long-term is anything longer.

Cost:

Many decisions involve 'cost' in terms of money. But there are many other costs. There is cost in terms of time and energy. There is cost in terms of hassle, anxiety, worry and stress (this might vary from person to person). There may be costs in terms of friendships and relationships to other people.

Every decision is a sort of purchase. We gain something but there is a cost. The danger is that 'doing nothing' seems to have no cost, but there is the hidden cost which is carried on. For example, deciding not to buy a house means that the cost of renting accommodation continues and also the cost of losing out on possible capital gains.

For a busy person the time and hassle cost may be even more important than the money. There is no limit to money but there is a limit to time. You can make more money but you cannot make more time.

Risk:

Risk is tied up with uncertainty. We can never be certain about the future, yet all decisions and choices are going to be acted out in the future.

Do we know the risks attached to each alternative? Can those risks be reduced? Are we prepared to accept those risks?

There are various sorts of risk:

SHORT-FALL: Things will fall short of what we hope. Things will not turn out as well as expected. Some of the contingency 'ifs' will not come through. A new house will obstruct the sea-view. The price of property will not rise as fast as expected.

HARM AND DANGER: If things do not work out you could be left much worse off. You may harm your health. You may damage your business. You may lose a reputation. You may harm someone else. You may get involved in costly litigation. Some of these risks may be very remote. Others may be almost likely. If you neglect your business for three years it is likely to suffer.

COST-OVERRUN: The cost in terms of money, time, effort and hassle may be far greater than you imagined. Had you known this in advance you would not have made that choice. Legal costs, medical costs, building costs, product development costs always tend to overrun. What estimates will you make for these overruns?

CIRCUMSTANCE CHANGE: Your health may change. Stock-markets rise and fall. Governments and tax laws change. Friendships change. Interests change. If your choice is a good one only in particular circumstances, how likely are those circumstances to continue?

FALL-BACK POSITION: Is there a fall-back position? If all goes wrong what do you do? Can you cut costs and walk away? What is the worst that can happen? You may not be able to tell what is the worst that can happen in terms of external circumstances but a fall-back position could limit your loss.

We try to minimize risk through more information, through fall-back positions, through hedging (balancing one risk against another) and through pre-testing alternatives. In the end we need to know the risk attached to each alternative and whether we are prepared to take that risk.

Trial and Testing:

In some cases 'trial and testing' is a very important part of the choice process. Some alternatives may be easy to test in advance. Others may require a total commitment. You can rent a house in order to try living in a faraway place. You can go to a party for a few minutes, in order to see if you like it. You may be able to borrow a car in order to test-drive it. It is not easy to test careers if a long period of study is required. It is not easy to pre-test a political decision.

Can we test this alternative? Is there a simple way we can try this out? An alternative that is easy to test may become more attractive than an alternative that cannot be tested.

SELECTION

What happens when we have gone through this check-list? We might have a clear winner. Some alternatives might have dropped out. We may have a short-list.

It is sometimes useful to make a mark against alternatives. One mark is for the most suitable on most counts. Another mark is for those alternatives which are less suitable but just have one strong point going for them.

You can introduce a new priority, a new criterion, in order to reduce the short-list further.

One useful procedure is to imagine you have chosen each of the remaining alternatives (on the short-list). You are now explaining to someone exactly why you made this choice. You will be surprised to find how feeble the reasons for your choice sound in many cases. You therefore have to admit that the choice of those alternatives would be largely emotional. There is nothing wrong with this provided you admit it – and accept the risk.

If the alternatives are all equally attractive, it should not matter which one we choose. But it does matter, because we are very reluctant to give up an attractive possibility. So the next thing you can try is to 'un-love' the alternatives. You take each alternative in turn and focus on the unattractive features (too much travel, too little time, hassle etc.). It is surprising how quickly perceptions can change. When alternatives no longer seem attractive it becomes easier to give them up – and make a decision.

FOUR CHOICES

You could make four choices instead of one:

THE IDEAL CHOICE: What is the nearest to this?

THE EMOTIONAL CHOICE (red-hat thinking): In spite of everything which alternative is the one you like best?

THE PRACTICAL CHOICE: Which alternative passes the 'check-list test' best of all? Which alternative is simply the most practical?

THE MINIMAL CHOICE: If you were lazy and wanted an easy life, which choice would you make?

If there is an alternative near the ideal choice, you would probably choose this. Otherwise it is a matter of personality. Some people should make the emotional choice and live with the consequences. For others the practical choice is best. In certain matters the minimal choice is right for some people (you may miss out on some gain but save a lot of trouble).

DESIGN

If you still cannot make a choice, you should set out to design some new alternatives. You could also try to re-design the alternatives that you have. It is time now for a creative effort. Think also of the things you could do using each alternative as a base. This is also a creative effort.

As a result of this design effort you may find that one alternative suddenly becomes very attractive. This is because this alternative, although not very attractive in itself, provides an excellent base for doing other things. But you have to imagine those other things.

Whenever choices and decisions become difficult on judgement grounds, it is time to use green-hat creativity. Instead of just looking at what 'is' we look at what 'can be'.

ANALYSIS PARALYSIS

If too much analysis has made a decision difficult, put on the red thinking hat and see what you 'feel' like doing. Only give up this choice if there are very good reasons against it (black hat).

SUMMARY

There are many situations which directly require choices and decisions. In addition most thinking processes come to a stage where there has to be a choice between alternatives (problem-solving, design etc.).

In the end all decisions and choices are emotional, but we should use our thinking to improve our perceptions so that our emotions can be usefully applied.

For minor decisions and choices there are simple procedures using the six hats or the attention-directing tools (C&S, PMI, OPV etc.).

For major decisions and choices there is a check-list procedure which includes: objectives and priorities; benefits; feasibility; difficulties and dangers; impact; consequences; cost; risk; trial and testing. There are some final selection processes. If this is not enough it is time for design and creative thinking.

EXERCISES ON DECISIONS AND CHOICES

1. What sort of decisions do you find difficult?

2. Is it better to have many friends or one good friend? Do a PMI on each of these alternatives. Give a conclusion.

3. Should young people be given a lot of spending money by their parents or a little? Do a C&S on these alternatives.

4. You are going to set up a pizza place. There are three alternative sites: downtown, highway, shopping mall. Use the following tools: AGO, FIP, OPV, C&S, PMI to make a choice.

5. A friend of yours has two alternatives. He (or she) can take a holiday job and earn money in order to buy a new tape deck. Or he (or she) can use some saved money to take a holiday with other friends.
What could he find under the following hats: red, yellow, black, green?

6. Your parents are trying to decide whether to buy a used car from a good friend or a new car. You are helping with their thinking. Check out both these alternatives for: feasibility, benefit, risk and consequences.

7. A company wants to get more productivity out of its workers. A consultant is called in and suggests the following alternatives.

... pay them more.
... sack the lazy, get new harder-working people.
... give the workers more training.
... reward productivity increases.
... give the workers more responsibility.
Do a full check-list assessment of each alternative, and choose.

8. What are the risks in lending money to a friend?

Third Review Section

All the thinking tools put forward in this book can be used on their own.

You can do a PMI.

You can ask someone to do a C&S or an OPV.

You can put on the red hat.

You can ask someone to switch from the black hat to the green hat.

The thinking habits put forward in this book can also be used separately.

You can watch out for the values.

You can pick out the broad idea.

You can examine the truth value.

You can check whether a conclusion has to follow from what went before.

This approach to the teaching of thinking skills is deliberate. It is based on many years' experience. Complicated structures look good on paper but do not get used. Even if a youngster just picks up and uses one or two tools from this book that will make an improvement in his or her thinking skill.

In these last sections I have, however, put forward some suggested structures for those who want to use structures. Older and more motivated students of thinking and those thinking about serious matters may want a more formal approach.

The purpose of a structure and the value of a structure is to enable us to do complicated things step by step. We follow the steps indicated by the structure instead of figuring out what to do at any moment. You are free to put together your own structures.

GENERAL-PURPOSE STRUCTURE

The five stages of the structure are given by the syllables: TO/ LOPOSO/GO.

TO: Purpose and objective of the thinking. What do we want to end up with?

LO: What we see when we look around. The information, the factors, the scene, the terrain. The input into thinking.

PO: The active, generative and productive stage of thinking. We produce alternatives, ideas and new ideas. Possibilities and possible courses of action.

SO: Selecting from the alternatives. Narrowing things down. Arriving at a specific course of action or conclusion or outcome.

GO: The action stage. Implementation. Plan of action. The steps to be taken. There must always be some action output.

Within each of these stages we can use thinking tools as we wish: for example CAF and OPV in the 'LO' stage; FIP in the 'SO' stage.

There is a visual diagram to reinforce the structure. This has the form of an L-shape. The vertical limb represents the input into the thinking. The horizontal limb moves forward into the future and suggests action. The corner position where the vertical changes to the horizontal limb is 'PO' and the generation of possible alternatives.

ARGUMENT AND DISAGREEMENT

This is the first of the special situations for which a structure is offered.

The basic approach is to lay out 'alongside each other' the two opposing views. This is done at four levels.

EMOTIONS: Red-hat thinking from each side.

PERCEPTIONS: The way each side sees the situation.

VALUES: The values for each side.

LOGICAL ARGUMENT: The logic offered by each side.

In order to lay out these opposing views there may be three steps:

1. These are my views.

2. I believe these to be the views of the other party.

3. What are the views of the other party?

Steps 2 and 3 can be interchanged if the other party is willing to state its views.

When the views have been laid 'alongside each other' – without challenge or argument – the following steps can take place.

COMPARISON: What are the points of difference? What are the points of similarity? Can these differences be resolved or removed?

DESIGN: Can the opposing views be brought together in a design that looks after the values of both sides? Can the apparent contradictions be reconciled?

TRADE AND EXCHANGE: If the design step does not work, there is an exchange or trading of values. Some value is given up in order to enjoy another value.

PROBLEMS AND TASKS

A problem is something that gets in our way. Problems present themselves. A task is something that you set up for yourself because you want to get somewhere.

In both problems and tasks there is a starting position and a place where we want to get – but we do not know how to get there.

The Problink™ method uses a basic diagram format. There is the starting position, then there is the route, and then there is the objective (or final position).

Starting with the objective we 'drop' down ideas or items. These may be sub-objectives or alternative definitions of the objective.

We then do the same for the 'route' area. We now 'drop' down broad ideas. These broad ideas cover ways we might reach the objective. These ideas may be very broad but may also be almost specific.

Next we move to the 'starting position' and 'drop' down elements or features that are to be found. This need not be a comprehensive analysis.

We now take any of these 'dropped' items and try to link it up with any other item. We can move in any direction. When we have formed a linked route that takes us from starting position, through route to the objective, we seek to turn the broad ideas into detailed ways of getting things done.

At the end we should have several alternative courses of action available.

There are various ways of assessing the alternatives. There can be a simple use of PMI or C&S. There can be yellow-hat followed by black-hat thinking. There can be a short check-list that considers: objective, feasibility, priorities, values and 'general assessment'. There can also be a full-scale assessment, as in 'decisions and choices'.

DECISIONS AND CHOICES

There are many situations which directly require a decision or choice as the thinking action. Many more situations (such as problem-solving, design, planning etc.) reach the stage where there are a number of possible alternatives and a choice between them has to be made.

In the end all decisions and choices are emotional even when they seem objective and neutral. The purpose of thinking is to allow emotions to act upon perceptions that are broad and clear.

The emotions of greed, fear and 'laziness' contribute to most decisions. It is worth asking oneself in every case what contribution these three emotions might be making. 'Laziness' includes a desire for a quiet life and low hassle.

For minor decisions and choices we can use a six-hats sequence.

RED HAT

YELLOW OR BLACK HAT (opposite to the 'feelings')

BLACK HAT (unless just used)

GREEN HAT (to overcome difficulties)

RED HAT (final feelings)

It is also possible to use the attention-directing tools. A PMI on its own or a C&S on its own provides a simple assessment. For a more thorough assessment you can use the tools in the following sequence:

AGO
FIP
OPV
C&S
PMI

For major decisions and choices there is time for a fuller assessment and this takes the form of a step-by-step check-list that is applied to each alternative in turn:

OBJECTIVE AND PRIORITIES: How well does this alternative meet the objective and fit the priorities? Perhaps an 'A' list for the alternatives that fully fit the priorities and a 'B' list for the rest.

BENEFITS: Yellow-hat thinking. What are the direct benefits for the decider or doer?

FEASIBILITY: Can this be done? Is it possible? Something may be feasible only with a great effort.

DIFFICULTIES AND DANGERS: Black-hat thinking. Difficulties in getting things done. Contingencies and 'ifs'. Actual dangers.

IMPACT: The impact of each alternative on life style, people, other projects, environment etc. Following the spread of the ripples of effect.

CONSEQUENCES: Direct look at the future in terms of immediate, short-term, medium-term and long-term effects. Covering these again even if they are mentioned elsewhere. What will follow?

COST: Not only in money but also in time, hassle, energy, effort, stress, anxiety etc., etc. What are my 'outputs'?

RISK: The need to assess the risk and to be prepared to accept the risk. Different types of risk: short-fall; harm and danger; cost-overrun; circumstance change; fall-back position or safety-net.

TRIAL AND TESTING: Can this alternative be tested? The possibility of trying out an alternative before full-scale commitment is a great advantage.

After the application of this check-list the choice may become obvious. If not, further items may be added to the check-list.

Sometimes the difficulty arises from a reluctance to give up alternatives that are all attractive. In such cases an effort is made to 'un-love' alternatives by looking at each of them in a negative light. This makes it easier to give them up.

One approach is to make four choices instead of one:

IDEAL CHOICE

EMOTIONAL CHOICE

PRACTICAL CHOICE

MINIMAL CHOICE (least effort)

The personality of the chooser will then decide which of these is best.

If selection is still not possible, there is a need for design and creative thinking. Existing alternatives may be modified. Alternatives may be combined. New alternatives may be generated.

Finally, if too much thinking seems to have confused the matter, it could be useful to apply a simple red hat. What do I feel like choosing? This is then followed by the black hat. Why not?

SUMMARY

Four structures have been put forward: general purpose; argument and disagreement; problems and tasks; decisions and choices.

For each structure the steps should be followed systematically, one after the other. The degree of detail that is required at each step will depend on the seriousness of the matter.

After going through the structure the answer, solution or conclusion may be obvious. If the conclusion is not obvious this is because there is no suitable alternative or you cannot decide between alternatives. There are two possible next steps:

1. Define the 'sticking point' or a new problem and think about that.

2. Use creative thinking to generate new alternatives or to modify existing ones.

The thinking cycle can repeat itself again and again. The outcome of thinking may be the definition of a new focus area or problem. Thinking about that may produce yet another focus area – and so on.

REVIEW EXERCISES

1. A girl (or boy) wants to paint her (or his) room yellow. Her mother wants the room to be blue. What sort of thinking situation is this? How should the thinking proceed?

2. Apply the TO/LOPOSO/GO framework to the following.
Fat people are tired of the bad image they have. They decide to have a campaign that 'fat is beautiful'.

3. A man promises to pay two young friends for painting the garden fence. When it is finished the man wants to pay only half the agreed price because he says the work has been poorly done. Use the disagreement structure to sort this out.

4. You have friends over all the time. Your parents think this is too much because they want some peace and quiet. Put down the perceptions and values on both sides. How could the argument be solved?

5. In some countries more and more people move from the countryside to the big cities, looking for work. The cities get impossibly large. What can be done about this problem? Use the full Problink ™method to tackle this.

6. In a competitive test you notice that several of your friends seem to be cheating. What alternatives do you have? Put down the alternatives, then use a sequence of the attention-directing tools to decide between the alternatives.

7. Do a full check-list assessment of the following alternatives for a nineteen-year-old boy (or girl):
... continue to live at home.
... share an apartment with two friends.
... rent a room on his or her own.

8. You find a wallet full of money in the street. The person you are with wants to keep it. You want to trace the owner. What thinking should take place?

PART FIVE

Newspaper Exercises

The following exercises are for those youngsters and families that have begun to enjoy thinking as a hobby. In these exercises there is an output that is concrete and visible. You can see how well you are doing.

1. THE TOWER

You are allowed just one sheet from a newspaper. That is to say a sheet that you pull out without cutting anything (normal folded sheet).

You are allowed a pair of scissors – but nothing else.

You are not allowed glue, pins, sticky tape or anything else.

The task is to make a tower that is as high as possible. This tower should be stable enough to remain standing under normal conditions for at least one hour.

Thinking:

What are the objectives? What are the problems? What tasks do I set? What are the alternatives here?

There is thinking needed for the design of the tower. There is thinking needed in order to do what you want with additional tools and materials.

When you have your stable tower, that is only the first step. You keep that tower – or at least record the height.

You should go back to the problem again and again. Each time you try to improve upon your performance. Can you make the tower even higher? Is there a limit?

Sometimes you will try to carry out the same design in a more precise manner. Other times you may want to change the design completely in order to get more height.

You will experiment and try things out. Not all the ideas will work.

Log Book:

If you really want to get the maximum benefit from this on-going exercise you should keep a 'log book' of your thinking. In this book (with dates) you note down your thinking: the problems; the difficulties; how you plan to overcome the problems; what happens; new objectives; priorities; alternatives etc.

2. THE ADJECTIVES

Very often we use adjectives to indicate what we feel about something. We might say that something is 'smelly' or that someone is 'careless'.

There are times when adjectives are used for objective description, for example a 'cloudy' sky or a 'yellow' wall.

Can we tell when adjectives are being used for objective description and when they are being used to indicate 'feeling'?

The exercise is to take a newspaper and to draw a circle (pencil, ball-point or colour) around each adjective that seems to you to be a 'feeling' adjective. You can look at the 'letters' page or the editorial or wherever you like.

The task is to see how quickly you can find twenty feeling adjectives.

The choice of adjectives can be discussed with a friend or parents. Try to make out those that are most obvious.

This exercise can be done again and again. Compare how much time you take on each occasion.

3. THE BRIDGE

This is another structural exercise, similar to the tower.

Again you take a single sheet of newspaper. You are allowed a pair of scissors but nothing else.

The task is to create a bridge between two supports. The two supports might be two piles of books placed some distance apart.

You now choose a weight. This could be a book or any other weight of about half a pound. This same weight is going to be used each time.

You now see how far apart you can put the supports. What is the maximum length of bridge that you can construct from the single sheet of newspaper? Each time the bridge must be capable of holding the chosen weight exactly at the centre of the bridge.

As you get better at the task you will find that you can make a longer and longer bridge. The bridge must be stable for at least one hour.

The thinking steps involved are similar to those involved in making the tower. The needs of the task are, however, different.

As with the tower you can keep a detailed log book of your thinking.

As with the tower you should measure the length of the bridge – from the edge of one support to the edge of the other support – and then try to improve this distance. The sheets must always come from the same size of newspaper.

4. HEADLINE STORY

Look through the headlines (big, medium and small) in a single issue of a newspaper. The exercise must be done on just one issue.

The task is to put together as many headlines as possible so that the headlines come together to tell some story. The story must make sense on its own. If you have to fill in gaps, the story is less successful.

See how many headlines you can put together in this way. The more headlines and the longer the story the more successful you have been.

You can repeat this exercise as often as you like. As you become better at it you will become better at seeing alternative meanings of headlines. You will find that you are able to put together longer strings of headlines.

If you cut out the headlines you can try them out in different sequences. You may get completely different stories.

5. THE CHAIN

This is the third structural task. This time the task is to construct a chain or rope that is as strong as possible.

As before you are allowed a sheet of newspaper and a pair of scissors and nothing else.

The length of the chain is set at six feet. The chain may hang from a picture hook or the top of the door, or be attached in any way you choose. From the point of attachment to the top of the suspended weight must be six feet.

What is the maximum weight that your chain will support? You can start off with a small weight and then increase this. You can use kitchen scales to find the actual weight you can suspend. The weight must be suspended for at least one hour.

The nature of the weight and the way you attach the newspaper chain to the weight are up to you. You are not allowed any more newspaper. You can make a loop of newspaper and pass something through the loop but you cannot attach sticky tape to the newspaper itself (or string or pins).

You measure progress by seeing how much weight a chain of the same length can be made to carry.

The thinking involved is similar to that involved in the tower and the bridge. This time, however, the task is different because it is a matter of tension, not of structural strength. Also the weight involved will be much heavier.

As before you can record progress in a log book.

6. PICTURE AND STORY

This exercise can be done with a single issue of a newspaper but it is also permitted to use more than one issue.

The task is to take a picture (photograph) from the newspaper and then to match it up with a headline. This can be any headline except the one that is properly attached to that picture.

Your combination of picture and headline may be serious or it may be funny. As far as possible the task is to get a funny combination.

You can keep a stock of pictures and of headlines and then try them out in different combinations. What is being exercised here is your perception, your imagination and your ability to find alternatives.

The Ten-Minute Thinking Game

You can have a discussion, a conversation or an argument. Although these involve some thinking, the ten-minute thinking game provides a framework within which two people can apply thinking in a more direct manner.

There is no winner or loser. The game is to be enjoyed by both players (a two-person game).

Ideally each section should be timed to last exactly one minute. The game can also be played in a more relaxed manner, in which case the timing does not have to be so exact. The game should, however, always be played briskly.

The two players are 'A' and 'B'.

A: says a single word (noun, verb or adjective).

B: gives a context, setting, scene or circumstance.

A: from the word and the setting creates a specific thinking task. This may be exploration, design, problem-solving, opinion etc. 'A' must clearly define the objective: 'I want you to end up with . . .'

B: explores the situation and comes to a definite conclusion, suggestion or solution.

A: does a quick PMI on the solution put forward by 'B'. The Plus points, the Minus points and the Interesting points.

B: comments on the PMI given by 'A'.

A: explores the subject and puts forward a conclusion, suggestion or solution.

B: does a PMI on the solution given by 'A'.

A: comments on the PMI done by 'B'.

B: over-all comment on the subject (was it a good one?) and the thinking (were there any interesting ideas?).

Total time: ten minutes, if each segment is strictly kept to one minute. If one stage takes less time, this can be added to the next stage. In other words, stage three should be over at the end of three minutes, stage seven should be over at the end of seven minutes, stage ten should be over at the end of ten minutes etc.

EXAMPLE

A: 'Cat'.

B: Setting of the jungle.

A: That suggests tigers. Problems of tigers being an endangered species. I want solutions to this problem.

B: Tigers are killed by hunters. We need a way of protecting tigers from hunters. My suggestion is to make hunting illegal and also to set up special tiger reserves.

A: Plus points – reduce the killing of tigers. Minus points – the tigers in the reserve might interfere with farming and the people. Interesting points – will the tigers stay within the reserves?

B: Some tigers in reserves have become man-eaters and do cause trouble.

A: If we want more tigers we should breed them. My idea is to breed tigers in captivity and then to release them into the jungle.

B: Plus – you could breed from the best quality only. Minus – the process would be much too slow. Interesting – the captive tigers could be trained to avoid hunters before they were released back into the jungle.

A: The process could be speeded up if female tigers were captured for a few days only and given artificial insemination and then released immediately.

B (overall comment): An interesting subject. Reserves are already being tried with success. Some good ideas, especially the idea of 'training' tigers to avoid hunters. There might even be ways of doing this in the wild.

The advantages of the game are the need both to generate ideas and also to assess ideas. At each point each person has a specified task that has to be done rapidly. This is good training in thinking that is focused and thinking that is disciplined. Instead of the drift of ordinary conversation or the point scoring of argument there is direct practice of various aspects of thinking.

SUMMARY

A two-person thinking game with a to-and-fro of thinking.

A subject is set up and each person generates ideas about that subject. These ideas are assessed.

One minute is allowed for each stage.

The game provides a fast-moving framework for the disciplined and focused practice of various aspects of thinking (task-setting; generating alternatives and solutions; assessment; comment).

The Drawing Method

This is a powerful and practical method of exercising thinking skills. I have used it for many years with children of different ages, abilities and cultures.

The method may be used with children as young as five years old and it may be used all the way up to adults. With the young children the drawing may be rather rudimentary and may need to be accompanied by explanation.

By drawing I do not mean 'art' or pretty pictures that simply describe some scene. The drawings are 'functional' drawings which show how something can be done. In that sense they are 'problem-solving', 'task-solving' or 'design' drawings. There is something to be achieved and the drawing shows how it can be achieved. The drawing may show how you might weigh an elephant. The drawing might show a machine to exercise dogs. There are two books of mine based on this method and giving the approach of children to different tasks: *Children Solve Problems** and *The Dog Exercising Machine.*†

WORDS AND PICTURES

Children are often limited in their vocabulary by their socio-economic background. If the vocabulary of parents is limited so will be the vocabulary of the children. But with drawing children are free. Anyone can look at a cat and draw a cat. The similarity of drawings across a wide range of socio-economic backgrounds suggests that this method of showing thinking is very useful.

Children often do not have the right words to describe a sophisticated concept – but they are capable of showing that concept in action. In one drawing of a 'machine to put people to sleep' the

* Penguin Education, Harmondsworth, 1972
† Cape, London, 1972

youngster showed a person on an inclined bed. Music, and a hammer
blow to the head, put the person to sleep. When the person fell
asleep he or she would slip down the inclined bed and the feet
would hit a switch which would turn off the music. The concept is
that of 'feedback control'. The child would never have been able to
describe the concept in those words.

With words it is often possible to waffle and to be vague. With
pictures this is not possible. You have to draw something. A parent
or teacher can point to a particular part of the drawing and ask:
'What is that?'

Pictures can often be produced much more quickly than a description
in words.

Pictures provide an organizing framework for the thinking of a
child. With words it is difficult to keep everything in mind as you
write it down. With a picture you can at once see what you have
already done and what you still need to do. If there are gaps you fill
them.

OPERACY

Operacy is the skill of doing, the skill of making something happen.
Education is usually reactive and descriptive because it is much
easier to put something in front of a student and then ask that
student to react. There are not many practical ways of teaching
operacy. Asking children to run projects or to get involved in making
physical objects is useful but it may be very time-consuming. A
drawing is very quick.

In a drawing a child has to put together experience, functions and
concepts in a concrete way in order to achieve an effect. There are
problems to be overcome and difficulties to be considered.

It is often surprising how comprehensive the thinking of children
can be in their drawings. There is a consideration of factors, of
consequences and of other people.

With a drawing a youngster often gets a sense of achievement that
is not present with a written description. The youngster feels: 'I
have found a way of doing this,' and 'this will work.' Whether or not
the concept would work in real life is not important at the moment –
it works in the drawing. This sense of achievement is motivating.

DISCUSSION

A drawing provides a good basis for discussion between a parent and a child. The drawing is there in front of both of them.

The parent can ask for clarification and explanation:

Tell me what that is?

What happens over here?

What is that for?

How does this happen?

The parent can also draw attention to problems and gaps:

How do we get the elephant on to the machine?

What happens if the dog does not want to run?

Wouldn't that be very painful?

Around each of these points a thinking discussion could take place. Ways of dealing with the difficulty could be suggested. Values can be introduced.

If a child draws a box and says 'It all happens in there', you ask for a drawing of the inside of this box.

The discussion can also be at the level of broad ideas and concepts. A child's drawing is usually a particular way of carrying out a concept. It is not easy to see whether the child had the concept first and then thought of a way of carrying it out (for example how to motivate the dog to run) or thought almost directly of a detailed way of carrying out the concept. In children's thinking concept and actuality may occur side by side.

The parent can draw attention to the concept and can try to extract the concept. Parent and child can then look around for other ways of carrying out the concept.

What are we trying to do here?

How else could we do this?

What about doing it this way . . .?

SUMMARY

Asking children to make simple line drawings is a practical and effective way of developing thinking skills. These are not 'art' drawings but 'operational' drawings. Each drawing shows how some task can be achieved or some problem solved. The method practises the skills of operacy and design: how do you bring together things in order to achieve some desired effect?

Pictures have many advantages over words as a thinking medium. Words are a communicating medium. Pictures are not limited by vocabulary or social background.

Pictures provide an ideal medium for thinking discussion between parent and child because it is possible to focus on any aspect of the drawing.

EXERCISES WITH DRAWING

A list of possible subjects is shown below. You can add your own. Always remember that the subject must set some task.

1. How would you weigh an elephant? (You might be a zoo keeper and you need to know how much medicine to give.)

2. Design a machine for testing cars. (So that all the faults would be found before the car was sold.)

3. Show a new way for washing windows in very tall buildings. (The windows get very dirty on the outside.)

4. How would you design a better bus? (Buses carry a lot of people but are not always comfortable.)

5. Design an underwater house. (So that scientists can watch sharks and other fish as they swim by.)

6. How could roads be made more quickly? (Making new roads is very slow and very expensive.)

7. Show how you would test a bridge. (Bridges get old and unsafe. We need to know if they are still safe.)

8. How would you stop people from driving too fast? (Fast driving causes accidents and injuries.)

9. How could you design a better table for meals? (Design a table that is specially suited for eating from.)

10. Show a new way of catching fish in the sea. (There are existing ways, can you find a new way?)

11. How would you put out forest fires? (Each year forest fires cause a lot of damage.)

12. Can you show a way of exercising people in their offices? (People have to work but need exercise too.)

Final Word

Teaching your children to think may well be the most important thing you can do for your children. They will be growing up to live in a complex world. Information, qualifications and professional skills will not be enough. They will have to be able to think things out on a business, professional and personal level. That is going to require a lot of thinking. It is better if that thinking is skilled than if it is moment-to-moment argument.

Teaching your children to think may well be the most important thing you can do for society and for the world. The future well-being of the world is going to require a lot of thinking both by experts and by ordinary people. There is going to be a need to think through problems and to look after values (environmental and others). Critical thinking will never be enough. We also need thinking that is constructive, generative and creative. There is also a need for better thinking in disputes and conflicts. The old adversarial methods are slow, wasteful and increasingly dangerous.

This book has sought to put forward some thinking skills. These are very simple but if they are learned and used effectively they can greatly improve thinking. This view is based on years of experience in this field at both adult and child level.

I believe that thinking is a skill that can be learned, practised and enjoyed. Once we can detach the ego from thinking and get past the *I Am Right – You Are Wrong* attitude, then thinking is a pleasure.

The book is concerned with 'operacy' and the thinking skills needed for getting things done. I feel that society has never paid sufficient direct attention to such matters. Traditionally thinking has been contemplative, analytical and critical. This can no longer be enough.

There may well be better ways of expressing what I have put forward in this book. It is always possible to find fault and to claim to have a better approach. In the end it is important to be practical – even if this is not perfect. The material in this book has been tried out over many years. From time to time armchair philosophers have claimed that these things 'cannot' work. Yet in practice they do work and work well. That is the important test.

I do not expect users of this book to remember and use every part of it. Even if only a few tools or habits are remembered and used, this will make a big difference. How often in your life do you pick up even a single habit or thinking method that can last you the rest of your life?

You can go back to the book again and again to take more from it each time.

Thinking is not intelligence, or information, or being right but an operating skill that can be improved. Whatever the existing level of thinking skill may be, that skill can be improved if we want to improve it. This book has been offered as a means of turning that 'want to' into a series of practical steps that can be taken. Destinations do not usually come to meet you – steps need to be taken in the direction of the destination. If you want to be a better thinker, this book offers some steps that can be taken.

A practical framework for practising and enjoying thinking is outlined in the Appendix.

Appendix: Thinking Clubs

The thinking clubs are separate from the rest of the book. No one has to set up or take part in a thinking club. The thinking-club structure is an opportunity for those who want to make use of the opportunity:

1. Single families or a joining-up of more families who want to have a more formal setting for going through this book and developing thinking skills.

2. Those who have learned the thinking skills in this book but realize that without frequent practice these skills deteriorate. Such people may also want to take their skills further (with other material of mine).

3. Those people who have come to enjoy thinking and want to have an opportunity to enjoy thinking as one might enjoy a sport or a hobby. It helps if there is a place, a time and other people.

4. Those who know that they will not have the discipline to learn and practise the thinking skills on their own – and also find it more enjoyable in a group.

5. Those who want to give a basis and a purpose to meetings that would otherwise be simply social.

PURPOSE OF THE THINKING CLUBS

Different people may have different purposes in setting up a thinking club, or joining one. The five main purposes are:

1. Learning and developing thinking skills in a deliberate manner. The direct learning of thinking as a skill.

2. Specific opportunity to practise thinking skills. This is to improve those skills, to prevent the skills deteriorating, and a direct enjoyment of thinking (as a sport or hobby).

3. The application of thinking skills to problems, tasks and projects. These can be of a personal nature, a practical nature or a remote nature. Both the exercising of thinking skills and the practical outcome have values.

4. A reason to meet and enjoy the company of others. Thinking provides an interesting and positive way of interacting with others. Instead of polite conversation there are frameworks for discussion.

5. A base from which others can be persuaded that thinking is an enjoyable skill, that thinking can be learned, that constructive thinking is important for the future well-being of the world.

ACTIVITIES OF THE THINKING CLUBS

The specific activities of the thinking clubs will be covered in more detail later in the section. They are:

1. Learning thinking skills.

2. Practising thinking skills.

3. Applying thinking skills to specific projects.

4. Applying thinking skills to personal or local matters.

5. Thinking about and discussing major issues.

The actual mix of these activities will vary with the composition and motivation of the members of a particular thinking club. For example a club with young members might want to concentrate on skill development. A club with active adult members may want to apply thinking to specific projects. A club with mainly senior members might enjoy discussion about world issues.

PRINCIPLES

In general the principles of good thinking that have been discussed in this book would form the basis of the thinking taking place in the thinking clubs. All the same, it is worth spelling out five fundamental principles.

1. The thinking must always be constructive in nature.

2. The thinking is directed towards operacy (skills of doing) and towards effective thinking. The purpose of the clubs is not philosophical contemplation.

3. There is a direct interest in developing and improving thinking skills. And not in showing how clever you are and how you can win arguments.

4. At all times the thinking must be enjoyable. The thinking must not be too complex or generate too much emotional stress.

5. The clubs will be based on my approach to thinking. This is very important, because the mixing-up of different approaches can create total confusion even where the different approaches have merit. In sport too many coaches create a mess.

It is possible to run thinking clubs on different principles. Anyone is free to do so. Good luck to you. I am putting forward my own suggestions here.

PRACTICAL MATTERS

The suggestions here are given as guidelines. They can be adjusted or modified according to circumstances or the nature of particular groups.

Discipline:

Because thinking is so free in nature, discipline is very important. Without discipline the clubs will quickly degenerate into opinion and argument sessions in which one or two people seek to impress the others. If this is what the group wants, the members of that group can enjoy it – but that is not what I mean by a thinking club.

The main discipline is that of time and focus. If there is a strict time discipline, the mind becomes disciplined about other matters. Time discipline means starting and ending at the specified time. It means sticking to set timings for the exercises. It means cutting off a discussion at the end of the time limit.

Years of experience have shown that time discipline in thinking enables people to think much more productively and much more rapidly. Without time discipline there is just waffle, drift and argument.